BUILD YOUR OWN CHRISTMAS MOVIE ROMANCE

Pick Your Plot, Meet Your Man, and Create the Holiday Love Story of a Lifetime

Riane Konc

ULYSSES PRESS

Published in the United States by:
Ulysses Press
P.O. Box 3440
Berkeley, CA 94703
www.ulyssespress.com

ISBN: 978-1-61243-944-0
Library of Congress Control Number: 2019942074

Printed in the United States by Versa Press
10 9 8 7 6 5 4 3 2 1

Acquisitions editor: Bridget Thoreson
Managing editor: Claire Chun
Editor: Lauren Harrison
Proofreader: Renee Rutledge
Front cover design: Malea Clark-Nicholson
Back cover design: what!design @ whatweb.com
Interior design and layout: what!design @ whatweb.com
Artwork: shutterstock.com

For Evan and Ramona

Contents

SCENE
1

MEET THE
HEROINE

"That's none of your business!"

Chrissy slammed her business phone down on her business desk and sighed. She looked around. Her entire desk was covered with business binders, business books (including the classic, *How to Business Your Way to the Top of Business*), and business supplies. One thing was for sure: She was a business lady. The phone rang again. She picked it up, shouted, "Business!" and slammed it back down. She simply had too much business to do to deal with all of this.

Chrissy pulled a hand mirror out of her desk drawer and examined herself. She was dressed the way she did every day: dark blazer, skirt, and extremely sensible heels—in fact, when she bought them, Chrissy had asked the shoe salesman to bring her the "heel equivalent of the woman at the bar who takes her friends' keys and is always reminding them to keep drinking water." That's how sensible they were. To complete her outfit, she wore her hair pulled back into a smart ponytail (not like a ponytail you'd wear for sports, but the kind of smooth business ponytail that business ladies can pull off). In short: the perfect outfit for doing business. She checked her makeup in the mirror—minimal, not so distracting that it would get in the way of business. Every eyelash in place. She took a deep breath. Today was going to be the day. Chrissy had started at Big Business Company ten years ago as an intern, and now, after years of thankless work—filing, sorting, synergizing, circling back on that email—it was finally happening. She was going to be promoted to junior executive in charge of business.

"I'm not a businessma'am," she whispered to her reflection in the mirror. "I'm a business, ma'am." It was what she always told herself when she needed to get pumped up.

Her phone rang again and she grabbed it in frustration. "Eve, I told you to hold all my calls," she snapped at her assistant through the line.

"Sorry," Eve whispered. "But it's your mom, so I thought you might want to make an exception."

Chrissy sighed.

Should Chrissy ...

 Take the call? *Start reading at the phone below.*

 Ignore the call and fantasize about her upcoming ski vacation? *Turn to page 17 and start reading at the skis.*

Chrissy knew what this was about. With a final groan, she said, "I'll take it on line one."

"Honey!" exclaimed her mother moments later. "It's so good to hear your voice."

"Hi, Mom," said Chrissy, bracing herself.

"How's work?" her mom asked.

"Busy with business, as usual," said Chrissy.

"Look, honey, I know you're busy, so I'll make this quick. I'm just finalizing all my meal prep for our big Christmas dinner, and I just wanted to confirm that you and Cole will be there with bells on."

Should Chrissy ...

 Agree to attend Christmas dinner? *Turn to page 9 and start reading at the wreath.*

 Tell her mom she won't be able to make it? *Turn to page 12 and start reading at the candy cane.*

BUILD YOUR OWN CHRISTMAS MOVIE ROMANCE

"Sure, Mom!" Chrissy responded breezily. "Of course we'll be there."

Her mind was racing. They would not be there. She and Cole had already agreed that they would not be attending this year's family Christmas dinner. They were planning on going skiing in the Swiss Alps. Plus, how had Cole put it? Oh, right: He'd said, "Family dinners? That sounds like something only lower-middle-class people do." Then he slicked his hair back with one hand, caught his reflection in a storefront window, and flexed his biceps for all the street to see.

"Wow," he whispered to himself. "I'm rich and smart and have good muscles."

Chrissy felt a pang then, something deep inside that said, "Maybe this isn't the world's ... best man?" But she pushed that feeling away. She adored Cole. So what if he called puppies plus-sized rats? He was handsome and successful and exactly who a businesswoman like her belonged with. And plus, she remembered, his comforter was custom-made out of hundred-dollar bills. And she mostly felt like this was a good thing? Right? Maybe best not to think about it.

"Oh, I'm so glad!" Chrissy's mom cried, interrupting Chrissy's thoughts. "I hadn't heard from you in a while, and I was beginning to wonder if you'd be able to make it at all."

"Of course we're coming," Chrissy said.

Why did she keep saying that? Cole was going to kill her. Maybe, she thought. Maybe there was a way to reschedule the flights and the reservations so that they could swing by Candy Cane Falls before leaving. They should have thought this through earlier. The annual dinner at her mom's house was not a surprise: It was, you know, annual. Why did they schedule the trip to fall exactly on Christmas?

Suddenly, Chrissy had a flashback, a hazy memory of herself saying to Cole, "Schedule it on Christmas, so we miss all of the festivities this year. Because I don't know if I've told you," she had continued, "but I hate Christmas." Cole had nodded. "I know. It's literally your

Tinder bio," he reminded her. "And you say it in your sleep. And you yell it when you're surprised. And it's your password to everything."

"Not everything!" Chrissy exclaimed. "My bank account password is 'IhateChristmas123!' because I needed to use numbers and a special character."

Then Cole had leaned in, cautiously. "Do you mind me asking?" he had said. "Why ... do you hate Christmas so much?"

"The candy cane harvest was huge this year, which is great news for the bottom line, but bad news for my aching back."

Chrissy slapped him across the face. Her eyes went dark, like a Christmas bulb that had also gone dark.

"You know I don't talk about that," she hissed. "It's my mysterious secret. It gives me depth."

"... and there will be three types of potato casserole," her mom was saying. Chrissy snapped back to the phone conversation. "And your aunt is bringing green bean casserole—her special recipe, with extra starbursts—and, let's see, Tom from the shoe repair shop is bringing turkey casserole, and I think Susan from the PTA is bringing bread casserole, and Gladys from next door has volunteered to make a wine casserole, so I think you're really going to like it."

"I can't wait," Chrissy said weakly.

"I'm relieved," her mother said. "You know I don't like to ask for help, but the candy cane harvest was huge this year, which is great news for the bottom line, but bad news for my aching back."

Chrissy's parents had been lifelong candy cane harvesters: When her dad died ten years ago, her mom had kept the business going on her own. If you're from a big city, you may not understand what that means. You probably think that candy canes arrive wrapped in plastic, ready for your minty enjoyment. Well, the secret that small town folks know is that there's actually quite a bit that happens before that delicious striped treat arrives in your big-city penthouse. And that's where candy cane harvesters come in. The way it works is, something gets planted in the ground (Chrissy wasn't sure), and then some kind of farming was done to it (Chrissy never paid attention), and then after some amount of time (Chrissy never listened when her parents explained), they were ready to not be in the ground anymore (Chrissy didn't know how). At the bigger, industrial candy cane farms, there were machines that would harvest the candy canes, bushel after bushel. But Chrissy's parents' farm was a small operation, and they had always preferred to do the work themselves. They always said you could tell the difference when a candy cane was hand-picked.

"And I hate to impose," her mother continued. "But even for a couple of days, it sure would be nice to have a few extra hands around here to help bring the harvest in."

Chrissy tried to imagine Cole pulling candy canes out of the ground. She couldn't do it. It was as absurd as imagining him at a Brooks Brothers outlet store.

"I can definitely see Cole pulling candy canes out of the ground!" Chrissy said.

They chatted for a few more minutes, and then Chrissy and her mother said their goodbyes. Chrissy hung up the phone and opened her work laptop to shoot off a quick email to Cole.

"Told my mom we would be coming home for Christmas … oops. Don't have the heart to tell her we'll be skiing instead … she was so excited that you were finally going to be able to make it. Couldn't bum her out. Do you want to tell her? Hahahaha, just kidding, but also maybe you should tell her. Kidding! Unless you want to. Talk later." She hit send.

Then, a minute later, a sinking realization came over her, and she slowly pulled up her sent messages folder.

And there it was at the top, that last email she had typed for Cole. But she hadn't actually sent it to Cole, she could see now with horror. She had accidentally sent it to the next "c" email in her address book: chrissysbestmomintheworld123@hotmail.com.

She started scrambling, looking for a way to un-send the message, when her mother's response email arrived.

"I'm sorry you feel like you can't tell me these things, but I understand that you and Cole have your own plans too."

Chrissy sighed in relief, then kept reading.

"And seeing as the sport of downhill skiing carried you for nine months, gave birth to you, and raised you, I understand why you would decide to spend Christmas with it instead of your mother. Love, Mom (not skiing)."

Chrissy groaned. She would have to call her mom later to apologize and explain, but right now, she just had too much on her mind.

Start reading at the *on page 20.*

Start reading at the on page 20.

"Actually …" Chrissy began slowly. "I've been meaning to talk to you about that."

"What is it?" her mother gasped. "Oh no, will you be late? Will you miss appetizers? Sometimes there's enough spinach dip leftover by the time the big meal comes around, but honey, you know there's no guaranteeing that."

"No," Chrissy said. "We won't be late."

"Oh, thank goodness," her mother breathed. "You said that, and I just thought, Santa's bells, the worst has come. This is the literal worst thing that has ever happened in my life—"

Chrissy started to interrupt, but her mother continued, "And *yes*, I am including the deaths of both of my parents, with whom I was very close. But it's all okay! You'll be there on time."

Just say it, Chrissy thought to herself. "Actually," she started again, "Cole and I won't be able to come … at all."

There was silence on the other line, then a bit of shuffling, and then, a faint, haunting melody started playing fuzzily through the phone speaker.

BUILD YOUR OWN CHRISTMAS MOVIE ROMANCE

Should the song coming through the speakers be ...

 A sad classic Christmas song? *Start reading at the red musical note below.*

 A sad contemporary Christmas song? *Turn to page 14 and start reading at the green musical note.*

 Just a regular sad song? *Turn to page 15 and start reading at the blue musical note.*

Chrissy listened for a few seconds.

"Mom?" Chrissy asked slowly "Are you playing me an instrumental version of 'What Child Is This?' Are you … trying to communicate your feelings by playing haunting mood music again?"

"It's not supposed to be haunting," her mother sniffed. "It's supposed to be sad. And as a mother, this is the saddest Christmas carol I can think of." In the background, the recorded orchestra swelled. "It would be one thing if the baby Jesus was a twin or a triplet—then you kind of understand the question, you know?" she continued. "But whenever I hear this song, I just think about the night you were born, watching you sleep in the hospital nursery, and even though there were other babies all around, I remember thinking: What child is this?

Please. That's my child, Chrissy, and I love her so much that I would *die* before I missed a holiday dinner that she had planned."

"That's what you thought the day I was born?" Chrissy asked. "Scheduling conflicts around future holiday dinners?"

"You just can't understand unless you're a mother," her mom explained.

Start reading at the *on page 16.*

It was an instrumental version of a song that Chrissy knew but couldn't quite identify. She closed her eyes for a moment, trying to place the melody. Suddenly, she groaned.

"Moooooooom," she said. "Please tell me this isn't the string quartet version of 'The Christmas Shoes.'"

"Well …" her mother started.

"You have got to stop forcing me to listen to 'The Christmas Shoes' whenever you want to guilt me into doing something," Chrissy said. "I mean it! It was bad enough when you insisted on playing it full-blast in the mall last year. We aren't allowed back in Famous Footwear anymore!"

"It was coming up on Mother's Day!" her mom exclaimed. "How else was I going to drop the hint that a pair of extra-white Skechers Shape-ups would be the perfect gift?"

"Any other way," Chrissy said. "You could have dropped that hint literally any other way."

"Point taken," her mom said. "I just think it's never a bad time to think about 'The Christmas Shoes' and the many lessons it contains. Mostly about how much our mothers love us and how nothing is promised …" she trailed off.

BUILD YOUR OWN CHRISTMAS MOVIE ROMANCE

Chrissy waited.

"… nothing is promised," her mother tried again. "And you never know which Christmas dinner might be … you know …" she trailed off meaningfully.

Start reading at the *on page 16.*

Chrissy's mom had a habit of playing mood music when she was trying to underscore the point she was making. Usually it was a sad Christmas song.

"Mom," Chrissy started, but then stopped. "Wait a minute," she said, listening. "Are you playing 'Casimir Pulaski Day' by Sufjan Stevens?"

"I am," her mother replied tersely. "I'm feeling sad, and this was the saddest song I could think of on short notice."

"It is a sad song," Chrissy agreed. "But beautiful."

"Well, that's his whole thing," her mom replied.

"You kind of just want to take care of him, don't you?" Chrissy asked. "I can't explain it."

"Speaking of taking care of things," her mom ventured, "I guess I thought about this song because I'm just so worried about how I'm going to take care of things around the house this Christmas without you."

Start reading at the *on page 16.*

"Come on, Mom," Chrissy groaned.

"It's tradition!" her mother protested. "What about our big Christmas supper? And snuggling by the fire on Christmas Eve? And besides, who's going to help on the candy cane farm if you aren't there? You would be so helpful to have around, and you know how demand gets to be around Christmas!"

"I'm sorry," said Chrissy, firmly. "But I'm getting older, and wearing sharper and sharper blazers, and I just care about New York City and business now. I think I'm starting to outgrow Candy Cane Falls. Don't you think it might be time to, you know, let some traditions go?"

There was silence on the other end of the line.

"Besides," continued Chrissy. "I'm about to be promoted to junior executive in charge of business, so I'm sure they'll be needing me at Big Business Company more than ever. I'm sure you can hire some Candy Cane Falls townie to help you with the candy cane harvest."

"Okay," sighed her mother. "I can see that I won't change your mind. But if your plans change, you know that there will always be room for you and Cole at the Christmas table. If I haven't died of heartbreak before then. And I probably won't," she quickly added. "But I'm also not saying it's impossible."

Chrissy sighed and changed the subject.

They chatted for a few more minutes, and then Chrissy and her mother said their goodbyes, and Chrissy hung up the phone.

Start reading at the *on page 20.*

"Tell her I'm out to lunch," Chrissy said.

"But it's 9 a.m.," Eve whispered.

"Then tell her I'm extremely hungry," Chrissy replied.

Eve hung up and Chrissy leaned back in her chair. If she talked to her mom, then that meant explaining that she would not be coming home to Candy Cane Falls for Christmas dinner like she did every year—that instead, she was taking a luxurious ski trip in the Alps with her very fancy business boyfriend, Cole.

She didn't like to brag, but Cole was very good at business. For example, he used a lot of hairspray. And he shopped at Brooks Brothers regularly, not just during their semi-annual sale. When Chrissy first met Cole, she took one look at him and thought, "That man has a boat."

And you know what? She was right.

When Cole had first tried to get her to skip the annual family dinner in favor of a long weekend of skiing, Chrissy had wavered for a while: On the one hand, she loved skiing, because it showed that she was rich. But on the other hand, she loved her mother because of biology. And she knew that her mom would be crushed if Chrissy missed the annual Christmas dinner. After all, it was the only time

> **When Chrissy first met Cole, she took one look at him and thought, "That man has a boat."**

during the year that she could ensure that Chrissy was eating carbohydrates instead of the business salads she relied upon in New York.

But Cole had convinced her with five simple words: "There's no Christmas in Switzerland."

"I don't think that's true," Chrissy replied at first, but Cole shushed her.

"No. Christmas. In. Switzerland," he repeated, smiling.

Then Chrissy smiled too. Because if there was one thing she hated more than anything in the world, it was Christmas. She didn't talk about why, because it was complicated and personal, and she was mysterious, and besides, she was too into business to deal with trivial matters like feelings and emotions. She just hated Christmas, and that was that. There isn't a huge, complicated story behind it that explains so much about her, and with which she must deal before truly being someone capable of accepting love. It's not that. So stop asking.

So if Cole could promise her a Christmas-free Christmas? Well that was just about the best gift of all.

So if Cole could promise her a Christmas-free Christmas? Well that was just about the best gift of all.

Just then, her phone rang again, and Chrissy grabbed it angrily.

"I said to tell her I'm out to lunch, Eve," Chrissy said sharply.

"I'm so sorry," said Eve through the speaker. "But it's not your mom this time. I know you don't want to be disturbed, but didn't you once tell me that if someone ever called for you claiming to be a radio DJ and saying that you had won a big prize, that I should immediately patch them through?"

"Yes," Chrissy said impatiently, "because even though there's a good chance that it's a scam …"

"… what if it *isn't* a scam," Eve completed the sentence for her. "Then you would regret it for the rest of your life. Exactly."

Chrissy sighed. "Did you call me just to talk about this?" she asked.

"Oh, no," said Eve. "Although it's been lovely chatting. I called because there's someone on line one claiming to be from W-BIZ, New York's number-one radio station for vaguely dissatisfied business professionals."

Chrissy squealed. "I love W-BIZ!" she cried. It might seem quaint these days to have a favorite radio station, but Chrissy couldn't help it: Even with all of the available streaming services, she was loyal to W-BIZ. Just the other week, as Chrissy was struggling through the world's longest Wednesday, the W-BIZ DJ had declared that it was time for a mid-week dance party, and then the station launched into one straight hour of commercial-free dance music: sixty minutes of "Drops of Jupiter" remixes, and it was—Chrissy sighed—exactly what she had needed.

"Well," Eve continued, "someone on the line is claiming to be DJ-CEO from W-BIZ, and he's saying you've won a big prize. It was hard to understand because he kept kind of giggling? But it sounds like you may have won an all-expenses-paid cruise on the W-BIZ Adult Contemporary Cruise Ship."

Chrissy high-fived herself. "DJ-CEO wants me to go on the 'All Aboard the Tita-Nick Cave and the Bad Seeds Cruise Ship' tour?!"

"That's the one," said Eve. "Sounds like they have a lot of fun things planned: spear-fishing with Hootie and the Blowfish, the lighthouse tour with Lifehouse, bird-watching with Counting Crows … they seem really committed to wordplay-based activities."

"Put him through," Chrissy said, sighing happily. There was definitely going to be a real DJ on the other line, she thought to herself.

"DJ-CEO, you're on with Chrissy," said Eve.

"DJ-CEO, it is an honor," Chrissy said into the mouthpiece.

"Hi, this is a real DJ from your favorite radio station," came a muffled voice on the other end, barely stifling its giggles. "I'm calling because, uh, you're the tenth caller, and you've won our big prize."

Chrissy paused for a long moment.

"Mom?" she said at last.

"No," giggled the voice, suddenly sounding more feminine than it had at first. "I mean, no," the voice tried again, now speaking in a false baritone. "No, this is just a real DJ, but your mom sounds like a wonderful lady who just wants the best for you."

Chrissy sighed.

"Hi, Mom," she said.

"Did you know it was me?" her mom said, speaking at last in her real voice.

"Of course I did," Chrissy lied. "I knew the whole time."

"It's hard to get through to you sometimes, you know," her mother continued. "I don't want to be cross, but that assistant of yours can be difficult!"

Say goodbye to that Vertical Horizon on-deck yoga class, Chrissy thought sadly to herself.

"Hey, Mom, I actually am a little busy right now," Chrissy said. "What's going on?"

"Oh, I'll get out of your hair soon," her mom said. "I was just hoping I could confirm with you that you and Cole would be at Christmas dinner."

Start reading at the *on page 12.*

Talking with her mom about Cole had reminded her: She had dinner plans with him that evening! They were celebrating their two-year dating anniversary, which, Chrissy reminded herself, was basically ten in business years. Cole had been acting strange lately, so when he asked if he could meet her for dinner at their favorite restaurant later that night, at once, she had realized: He was going to propose. All of the late nights, the secretive whispers, the volatile moods ... suddenly it all made sense: He had been ring shopping late at night and stressed about making the proposal perfect! It was so Cole—almost as Cole as changing the password on his phone and laptop so she couldn't access them anymore. Probably because they were full of pictures of the ring!

Tonight! It was really happening! She almost squealed in delight just thinking about it.

SCENE

2

BLUE
CHRISTMAS

Eve tapped on the door. Chrissy waved her in.

"They're ready for you in the conference room," Eve said.

By "they," Eve of course meant Janet and Tad, Chrissy's bosses. Chrissy was due for a promotion, and when Janet scheduled this meeting, Chrissy knew exactly what it was for: They were going to announce her new position as junior executive in charge of business. Chrissy was always assuming the outcomes of things, and this would prove to be an unequivocally good thing.

What would she do with the raise that would come with the promotion? Being a junior executive surely came with perks. A company car, maybe, or access to the executive-level dining room. But one thing was for certain: She had definitely earned this promotion. All those late nights and weekends, missing more family events than she could count, because she wasn't good at counting. Well, this would make up for it, she told herself. The first thing she'd buy with her raise would be a really nice gift for her mom, to make up for having to miss Christmas dinner.

All that time, and it was finally happening. She looked at herself hard in her hand mirror. "Chrissy," she said to her reflection. "You are getting a raise."

"Chrissy, you are not getting a raise," said Janet, after pleasantries had been exchanged. "I could see that look in your eye when you came in, and ... look, I'll get right to it. I'm afraid this meeting is not good news. Your position is being terminated, effective immediately."

"You can take until the end of the day to pack up your things," said Tad.

"It's nothing personal," Janet added. "It's simple dollars and cents. Which is to say, we want more of them. Your position just happened to be the next one on the chopping block."

Chrissy nodded in a daze and stood up. She ... was ... fired. She was fired? Starting to feel woozy, she leaned against the wall to steady herself.

Should Chrissy ...

 Accept her termination gracefully and leave? *Start reading at the dove below.*

 Make a big scene? *Turn to page 25 and start reading at the anger icon.*

"I … understand," Chrissy finally found a way to say. She straightened up. Be dignified, she thought to herself. Being a business lady is about dignity, and leaning against walls is *not* dignified. Unless you're inside the Leaning Tower of Pisa, in which case it kind of all cancels out, she reminded herself. She was always forgetting about that exception.

Tad and Janet were looking at her sympathetically. I don't need your pity, Chrissy thought. I'll show you that I'm fine.

"Just so you know," Chrissy continued, "I'm actually fine."

"Good—" Janet started.

"Actually, I'm *amazing*," Chrissy went on. "Fantastic. Spectacular. Superior. Prodigious. Awe-inspiring." It was a good thing she had read the "A" section of her thesaurus this morning.

"And," Chrissy went on, "I just want to let you know that I hold no hard feelings. You're just doing what you had to do. Honestly, I would have done the same thing!"

"Now, Chrissy," Tad said, holding up his hand, "there's really no need."

"I'm fine," Chrissy said brightly. "Slender. Small. Thin. Gossamer. Minute. Delicate."

Tad and Janet looked confused. Oh no, thought Chrissy. Wrong kind of "fine." Best to make a dignified exit.

"Jan. Tadet," she said, nodding as they tilted their heads in confusion. "Good day."

Start reading at the on page 29.

Chrissy stared at Tad and Janet, a simmering rage threatening to rise to the surface. Look at them, she thought with disgust. With their faces and their hair and their knockoff $2,000 suits. And their names! Those names! What kind of names are Tad and Janet?

"Uh, a family name?" Janet said.

"My mom liked baby frogs," Tad added.

Whoops, Chrissy thought. She must have said that last part out loud. Then, again, the rage. Tad. Janet. Fired. She glared at them, and then, in a burst of strength, grabbed the conference room table and flipped it over with a loud roar.

Well, sort of. She did grab the conference table with both hands, and she did *attempt* to flip it over, but it didn't work, so she just stood there, grunting, trying to pull the desk up toward her.

"It's nailed to the floor," Tad said quietly, as Chrissy's face turned redder and redder and a large forehead vein revealed itself.

Fine. If she couldn't flip a table, she could do something else. She grabbed the two closest three-ringed binders, threw them to the ground, and started stomping on them.

"Should we get security?" Janet murmured to Tad.

"No," Tad said slowly. "I think she'll tire herself out."

When Chrissy realized that her tantrum wasn't getting her the attention she expected, she straightened up and adjusted her suit jacket.

"Well," she said. "You can be assured you will be hearing from my lawyers about this." She didn't know what she would get a lawyer about, but it seemed like the sort of thing one should say in this type of situation.

With that, she turned and walked out of the conference room. But as she marched toward the lobby, she heard a muffled conversation coming from behind another office door. She stopped to listen: It seemed impossible, but she could have sworn that she had just heard someone say "Candy Cane Falls."

Should Chrissy ...

 Stop to eavesdrop on the conversation? *Start reading at the cup below.*

 Continue making her grand exit? *Turn to page 28 and start reading at the skate.*

Chrissy tiptoed closer to the door, trying to make out what was being said inside. There was almost no chance that someone in that room was talking about Candy Cane Falls: What were the odds that anyone in this building had even heard of her hometown? Chrissy wondered. But it didn't matter; she needed to know for sure. She pressed her ear against the door and listened hard, but all she could make out were muffled voices. Every person in the room sounded like the teacher on *Peanuts*, Chrissy thought to herself. Then, suddenly distracted, she thought, I bet Charlie Brown would have really benefited from a SAD lamp. But then again, Chrissy reminded herself, I would probably feel depressed too if I were a six-year-old experiencing male pattern baldness. Then, she remembered: She was trying to eavesdrop. How was she going to do it?

She was going to need some way to amplify the sound, Chrissy realized. There had to be a way, she thought. There had to be! Then suddenly, she gasped. "The One After Joey and Rachel Kiss"! Episode 1, Season 10 of the former hit NBC show *Friends*! Of course! How did it take her this long to remember? She shook her head, almost laughing. How could she forget about that infamous episode in which the gang is in a Barbados hotel room, struggling to eavesdrop on Ross and Charlie in the other room, when Monica suggests putting a glass cup up against the wall to listen through so that they could hear more clearly? Chrissy clapped her hand against her forehead. The answer had been right there all along! And they say that *Friends* hasn't aged well, she thought, rolling her eyes. Could they *be* any more wrong?

Chrissy sprinted to the breakroom and rushed back with a coffee mug in tow. She pressed it against the door and leaned in closely to listen. Still, even with the mug, she could only make out bits and pieces of the conversation: excited … rich … Richard Munneybaghs … funding … land … condos … Candy Cane Falls … small town … ornament shop … father figure … single mother … lease … beloved … Declan Halls … bulldozer … eviction … wrecking ball … townspeople … outcry … muwahahahaha … condos … money … perfect … talk soon … great meeting … goodbye …

And with that, someone pulled the door open and Chrissy tumbled face first into the office, the mug falling to the carpeted floor with a soft thud and rolling away.

A man with a pencil-thin moustache and a full tuxedo stood looking down at her in confusion. Chrissy stretched out and snatched the mug from the ground. "Like I always say, don't talk to me until I've had my coffee!" she cried nervously, holding the mug up by way of explanation. Then she scrambled to her feet and sprinted out of the office and down the hall.

Oh well, she thought to herself as she rushed toward the lobby. I guess I'll never be able to even sort of piece together what that conversation was about.

Start reading at the *on page 28.*

There was no way that anyone in New York—much less anybody in Big Business Company—would have any reason to be talking about Candy Cane Falls, Chrissy decided. She must have misheard. Maybe there was just a new associate named Mandy Laine Smalls? Either way, she wasn't going to worry about it. She turned away from the door and headed out through the lobby toward the elevators.

Start reading at the  *below.*

As she reached the middle of the lobby, she turned on her heel to face her coworkers, some of whom were peeking out of their offices to see what the commotion had been. "I would just like to say," Chrissy said loudly, so everyone could hear. "That certain people here are a disgrace to the very concept of good business. Business is good, but they—they are the opposite of good, and so they are the opposite of business. I came to this city to get away from Candy Cane Falls and to learn what a stiletto is, and guess what? I've done one of those things."

She took a deep breath.

"And to those certain people in this office who aren't worth the weight in their weighted tape dispenser, I would just like to say, I hope that every day of your life is like Christmas!" With that, she stepped into the elevator and closed the door.

The lobby filled with confused whispers.

"She sounded so mad, but then the end of her speech made it seem like she wanted good things to happen to us?"

"No, man, you forgot: Chrissy hates Christmas, so having every day be like Christmas would be, to her, the ultimate punishment."

"Why does she hate Christmas?"

"No one knows. It's her most mysterious secret."

"Even more mysterious than that ring of hers with the royal insignia we found on the floor that one day?"

"Maybe not as mysterious as that. There are a lot of implications there. But I'm not sure that we'll have the time or space to explore them."

As they spoke, the elevator dinged and the doors opened. It was Chrissy again.

She cleared her throat.

"I have … forgotten to clear out my desk," she said. "And honestly I have like, all of my stuff here, so …"

She trailed off.

"Well then!" she said brightly, and then marched into her office and slammed the door.

Start reading at the (swan) *below.*

Chrissy stayed in her office with the door shut behind her all day, absent-mindedly clearing off her desk and shoving her office decorations into old printer boxes. She glanced down at the wooden sign that read, "Live. Laugh. Love." Would she ever remember to do those in the right order? She flipped through her customized calendar, with the entire month of December missing. Would she ever have the strength to rip a piece of paper out of a calendar again? She rolled up the poster with a kitten hanging on a tree branch under text reading, "Hang in there." Would she ever find someone to explain that poster to her?

Fired. Fired? She said it so many times the word began to sound strange. Like "fired," but weird. "Fired, fired, fired," she whispered. Minutes slipped away, and then hours, until suddenly, she remembered: Her dinner plans! Nothing could distract from a bad day better than an anniversary dinner with Cole … and whatever he had planned. Chrissy smiled despite herself. She looked at her left hand. This would be the last time she saw it without a ring. She picked up her box of belongings and marched out of the office with confidence. *Good riddance*, she thought. It was no longer just a Green Day song that she connected with way too much as a junior in high school. She was done with Big Business Company, and that was fine. She would have more matrimonial things to worry about in the near future anyway. Business would just get in the way.

❄ ❄ ❄

"I feel like business has just gotten in the way," said Cole apologetically that night over dinner. "I travel, you work those crazy hours … come on, Chrissy, I can't be the only one feeling like this. We've been practically over for months."

Chrissy nodded dumbly. This is not how she had expected tonight to go. A waiter stopped by the table.

"More wine for the lady?" he asked.

"Wine is … more … good, fine," Chrissy muttered. She was in shock.

"I'll always love you, Chris, you know that," Cole continued. "But truthfully, I just don't know if a monogamous relationship is even for me! It's not natural, for one thing. Name one animal in all of nature that's monogamous—"

"Swans. And wolves," said Chrissy quietly.

"Oh," said Cole. "Well, I guess—"

"Also gibbons. Beavers. Shingleback skinks."

"Okay, I get the point—" Cole interjected.

"Barn owls," she said, her voice growing louder. "Bald eagles. French angelfish. Schistosoma mansoni worms!" she yelled. The entire restaurant grew quiet. "*Schistosoma mansoni worms, Cole!*"

Should Chrissy ...

 Throw her wine in Cole's face? *Start reading at the wine glass below.*

 Try to win him back? *Turn to page 32 and start reading at the martini glass.*

Chrissy picked up her glass, newly full of red wine. The expensive kind, because of all their business money. Back in Candy Cane Falls, they drank dumb, simple things like apple cider and hot chocolate and—Chrissy gagged—water. Lower-middle-class drinks. This wine wasn't for someone whose idea of splurging was to go to T.J. Maxx without a coupon. This wine was for *upper*-middle-class people. She paused for a moment, and then tossed the wine directly into Cole's face.

He sputtered and grabbed for a napkin.

"What about the Alps, Cole?" Chrissy said. "We were going to go to Switzerland and ski! I already bought my tickets!"

"I'll reimburse you," Cole mumbled.

"*That isn't good enough*—oh, wait, wow, really? Okay, that's a relief, honestly, because it was just going to be like, one other stressful thing, so I guess thank you, but also you can definitely rot in hell, but I do appreciate it," Chrissy said.

Cole nodded.

"I'll always love you Chrissy," he said. "Just not in the way where I … want to be around you. Does that make sense?"

Chrissy grabbed a water glass and threw it in Cole's face. Nothing happened. The glass had been empty.

"Oh," Chrissy said, examining the glass. "Oh, I see. I thought I couldn't see the water because water is clear, but now I see that it's because it was empty." She picked up a dinner roll and threw it at him instead.

"Goodbye, Cole," she said. "Call me if you ever reconsider monogamy."

Start reading at the *on page 35.*

Chrissy took a deep breath and lowered her voice. She had to remain calm.

"Cole," she said. "You don't mean this. You don't really want to lose everything we have, do you?"

Cole sat silently and shrugged.

Chrissy sensed an opening and pounced.

"Think about it," she said. "Friday martinis. Saturday brunches. Sunday Soylent shots. Our weekend walks through the city where we chant, 'I'm so glad I don't live in a small town!'"

"We have been through a lot together," Cole admitted.

"Yes!" said Chrissy. "We survived our favorite Italian place becoming an Italian-*fusion* place. If we can survive that, we can survive anything, right?"

Cole closed his eyes and rubbed his forehead. "I have to think," he mumbled.

BUILD YOUR OWN CHRISTMAS MOVIE ROMANCE

Chrissy kept going.

"Without me, who are you going to yell at waiters with? Who is going to help you decide which of your nineteen different black suits you should wear to work? Who's going to tell you there's gold foil stuck between your teeth when you don't want it there, or that there *isn't* gold foil stuck in your teeth when you do? Who's going to fill all our water bottles with vodka? Who's going to fill all our vodka bottles with stronger vodka? And who's going to fill our stronger vodka bottles with sand?"

Cole looked up.

"I love you, Chrissy," he said. "I really do. And everything you said—I love that. I love belittling waiters with you, you know that. I love writing snotty notes on the line for the tip instead of an actual tip. When I was a kid, I never thought I'd have the kind of relationship where I could make working-class people who are doing a difficult job cry … but with you, I had that."

"Have that," Chrissy corrected. "Have."

Cole kept on. "But we've been in a stalemate for a long time. We hardly ever talk except to send each other dollar sign emojis."

Chrissy's eyes were filling with tears. "To show you that the only thing I love more than you is money," she whispered.

"Yes," Cole said. "And please know that no matter what happens between us, I will always love you slightly less than money."

> *"I just think our relationship has run its course, and I would do anything to fix it except put in the time and effort it would take to make that happen."*

Chrissy nodded, tears streaming down her face, and mouthed, "Me too."

"I just think our relationship has run its course," Cole said. "And I would do anything to fix it except put in the time and effort it would take to make that happen."

"Please," Chrissy said, getting down on her knees. "I'm begging you. Please, Cole. Stay with me until at least after the Alps trip. If we don't go to Switzerland, I'll have to go home to Candy Cane Falls, and everyone there hates me just because I snap my fingers at waiters and because my pajamas are technically high heels and a pencil skirt. Before I left Candy Cane Falls, do you know what I thought a pencil skirt was?" Chrissy asked, tears springing to her eyes.

"What?" asked Cole.

"I didn't. I never even thought about pencil skirts at all," Chrissy wailed. "Please just let me come on the trip with you. Please don't make me go back to that place by myself for Christmas."

"I just don't think that's a good idea," Cole said. "I think I need to take this trip myself in order to do the whitest thing possible, which is to try and find myself while skiing. Besides, can't you just tell your mom you can't come home?"

"I'm from a small town," Chrissy said, glaring. "Where my appendix is supposed to be is just a giant well of guilt. I won't be able to lie to her. If she knows we aren't going on the trip anymore, then I'll have to go home. And oh, God," she gasped. "I bet they won't even have a place that delivers foie gras sushi. I'll have to order it for ... pick up." She started wailing again.

"Hey, I still have those skis you personalized for me," Cole said.

"You mean the solid-gold ones I decoupaged with pages from *Who Moved My Cheese*?" she asked.

"Yeah," said Cole.

"You know, I never told you, but I was going to add a small inscription on the bottom," Chrissy said. "It says, 'Small towns can suck it.' It was going to be my Valentine's gift to you."

Cole wiped a tear from his eye. "Thank you," he said, sincerely. "You know how much that means to me. But now," he stood up, "it's time for me to go find a woman who's more conventionally attractive than you."

Chrissy started to protest, but Cole cut her off. "Look, Chrissy. I'm in my business prime. I mean, look at me: I'm wearing a fitted navy suit and wingtip leather shoes, but my pants are tailored to be just short enough to reveal that I'm *also* wearing socks that are wacky colors! I've made it, Chrissy: I'm finally rich enough that I can make brightly colored socks a personality trait! And best of all," he leaned in closely, "I just finished listening to a Malcolm Gladwell audiobook, so I'm ready to appear much more interesting and smart than I actually am. Goodbye forever."

He walked away from her, through the door, and out into the street.

Chrissy waited a minute after he left, and then drained both of their glasses of wine.

Start reading at the  *below.*

On the cold walk home, she dialed her mom's number. She picked up on the first ring.

"Mom?" Chrissy said tearfully. "The ski trip is cancelled. Tell everyone I'm leaving the big city, with all its plexiglass and pigeons. I'm coming to the place where buildings are short and the birds are ducks. I'll ... I'll be coming home to Candy Cane Falls for Christmas after all."

THE
MEET CUTE

$\mathcal{The}$ sign on the side of the road said, "Welcome to Candy Cane Falls," and Chrissy's Uber driver slowed as he drove past to admire it. Decked out in an explosion of blinking lights, it was festive, but still—it was nothing compared to the town itself. The driver whistled as he pulled onto the main street, staring out the window at the winter wonderland that was Candy Cane Falls in December.

"Candy Cane Falls may be a small town," Chrissy said robotically, repeating something she'd heard a hundred times from her mother. "But there's nothing small about the way we do Christmas."

The car screeched to a halt to let three reindeer pass. The driver looked back at Chrissy in shock.

"It's just a small-town thing," said Chrissy. "Small towns, as I understand them, are just full of reindeer."

The Uber driver studied his phone. "Hmm," he frowned. "The GPS isn't finding me. Is there no service out here?"

Chrissy laughed. "Well," she said, "Candy Cane Falls is an old-fashioned place. I remember a few years ago they tried to update the technological infrastructure, but everyone was so upset, and there were so many protests, that they finally had to scrap the project. And to think," she said, shaking her head, "of all the good those cans strung between windows could have done for the people of this town. But I guess they just weren't ready."

"Any chance you can direct me to your house?" he asked.

"Sure," said Chrissy, then she paused.

Should Chrissy ...

 Take him straight to her house? *Start reading at the mitten below.*

 **Take him on a tour through town first?** *Turn to page 39 and start reading at the moose.*

"I can get you there," Chrissy said. "It's pretty easy. Just drive one mile past the Christmas trees, turn left when you hear the magical tinkling in the air, go another half-mile down the boulevard of memories, turn right when you see the carolers' graveyard, and when you get to the end of the road, follow your heart," she recited, remembering how her mother had always described the path to their home.

Her driver stared at her.

"Uh, west," Chrissy said. "Head west."

"Hey," Chrissy said, after a few minutes of driving, "I never asked your name."

"I know," said the driver.

Five full minutes passed.

"Evan," Evan said suddenly. "My name is Evan. At first I thought you were just stating a fact, like, 'Oh, a fact about me is I never asked your name,' but it just occurred to me that you were, you know, asking."

Chrissy nodded.

"It was confusing because it was a question without a question mark," Evan continued.

Chrissy nodded again.

"I'm going to keep driving now," Evan said. "While being named Evan."

Chrissy nodded once more, this time hiding a smile.

Start reading at the  *on page 45.*

"Actually," Chrissy said. "Let's take the long way. I want to show you Candy Cane Falls."

"I thought on the drive down you said you hated Candy Cane Falls," her driver said. "That it was a 'Podunk holiday mess that didn't even have one functioning stock exchange.' And then you said, 'By the way, I hate Christmas,' and gazed out the window mysteriously and wouldn't talk for the next hour."

"No, you don't understand," said Chrissy. "I want to show you Candy Cane Falls sarcastically. So that I can at least know that some other sane person from the outside can see what a ridiculous, worthless place this is and how few tourists there are to shove past on the sidewalks."

Chrissy sighed. She loved shoving past tourists on sidewalks. In fact, she could go for a good sidewalk shove right now. Maybe someone wearing a fanny pack. But of course, this was Candy Cane Falls, and there were no tourists to be found.

"Now this," Chrissy said, pointing out her window toward a small building decorated to look like a gingerbread house, "is City Hall." She leaned out the window, seeming to be searching for something. "Ah! There he is," she said. "Just right over there is our mayor."

Her driver craned his neck to see. "You mean that short guy standing behind that moose?" he asked.

"No," said Chrissy.

"You mean that woman in the power suit trying to walk in front of that moose?" he asked.

"Not her," said Chrissy.

"You mean that old guy who doesn't seem to realize that he's about to walk into that moose?" he asked.

"Not him," said Chrissy.

There were several seconds of silence in the car.

"It's the moose," he finally said, quietly.

"It's the moose," Chrissy repeated. "He's been mayor for something like six terms so far, but you have to remember, that's in moose years. Actually, that makes it worse. Keep driving!"

"This is the main drag," Chrissy said, when they pulled into the downtown, minutes later. "Let's see. We've got a hot chocolate shop, and a Christmas cookie shop, and a muffin shop, and a high-end candy cane shop, and a shop with furs and robes and tiaras, just in case someone in town ever falls in love with a mysterious stranger, and he turns out to be a royal and she needs to quickly look the part because his mother, the queen, is arriving today, and she must make a good impression—the future of Galdovia depends upon it!"

"You might also be surprised to find that we have a small technical school here," Chrissy continued. "You can learn useful trades like reindeer shoeing or snowshoeing or shooing away anyone who says they don't love Christmas! But that last one is more of a certificate program."

She pointed out the other window. "And over there is the Contests, Contests, Contests warehouse. It's the perfect place to go if you suddenly find yourself in a situation where you need to win some sort of baking contest to save your parents' farm or to raise money for a sick child or to prove to yourself that even though you're a widower, you can at least still … I don't know, bake cookies or something. Basically, they have anything you might need there: any aprons or cooking supplies or trophies or

> *"It's the perfect place to go if you suddenly find yourself in a situation where you need to win some sort of baking contest to save your parents' farm."*

prewritten motivational speeches you can give to yourself in the mirror before the big day, the day that you win the farm back and finally earn Dad's respect, although of course he'll tell you that he always respected you, he just didn't know how to show it. 'Aw, Dad,' you'll say, patting him on the shoulder, realizing you don't know what to say, but then your goofy younger brother will run into the kitchen, chuck a Christmas cookie at Dad's face, and yell, 'Food fight!' and you'll both look at each other like, 'Are we doing this?' and then you both shrug, like, 'I guess we're doing this!' and you both laugh and scoop up your own Christmas treats and hurl them at each other long into the night. This will somehow make up for a childhood devoid of paternal affection, and next year, guess who the judge of the cookie contest is? That's right, dear old Dad."

Her driver opened his mouth once or twice, but no words came out.

"Basically I'm just saying you could get that stuff there," Chrissy explained. "Anyway, that's the whole downtown. Now here on the way out," she said, pointing out the window, "is lonely Kris. He's always just kind of sadly walking around alone outside the shops, like he's just begging someone to ask if he's okay."

"Have you ever thought to ask?" the driver asked. Then, he peered out the window.

"Wait, are you talking about that big guy in the red sweatshirt with white piping?" he asked.

"Yep," said Chrissy.

"With the big white beard and black boots?" he asked.

"That's Kris!" she said brightly.

"Carrying that huge burlap sack?" he asked.

"Yes," Chrissy said impatiently. "You got it. That's Kris. I only pointed him out to you because if you ever run into him, you might get the vague sensation that if you only stopped to talk to him, to treat him like a human being, great mysteries and secrets might be revealed unto you, and you might learn a valuable lesson about outward appearances and inward beauty. But you should ignore that feeling because, like I made a point to say, it's just lonely, friendless Kris, and you don't need to worry about him. What do you think will happen if you

do? You think you're going to learn some kind of important lesson about the inherent value that exists in every person, no matter what difficult circumstances they find themselves in?"

"What does his burlap sack say?" the driver asked, squinting. "'Good … boys … and … girls … see … beyond … the surface?'"

"I can't imagine that it has any important meaning or that it's relevant in figuring out Kris and his whole deal," Chrissy said. "Things are always exactly as they seem, and North Pole magic isn't real."

As she spoke, she heard a faint tinkling sound outside, like tiny bells.

"Did you hear that?" she asked her driver.

"Hey," he said slowly. "Do you maybe want to pull over and say hi? At least see if he needs something?"

Should Chrissy …

 Pull over? *Start reading at the apple below.*

 Keep going to her mom's house? *Turn to page 45 and start reading at the Santa hat.*

"Fine," Chrissy said. "Pull over. Since you're so obsessed with him."

"I'm not obsessed. You know what, never mind," he said, pulling the car to the side of the road. "Let's just go say hi."

"Hey," Chrissy said, after a few minutes of driving. "I never asked your name."

"I know," said the driver.

They continued in silence until they reached Kris. His eyes lit up when he saw them.

"Hello!" he cried. "How nice to see two of my favorites! I'd been hoping you would say hello. You're as 'nice' in person as I always suspected." He did finger quotes when he said "nice."

Chrissy shot her driver a look that said, "See? I told you."

"Hi," said her driver, sticking out his hand. "I'm Evan. Nice to meet you."

"Evan, hmm?" said Kris. "Sounds a lot like Elfin, if you ask me." He winked.

Evan grinned. "Sure, I guess!" he said. "Hey, is there anything we can get you, Kris? We're happy to call someone to pick you up, if you need, or even grab a bite to eat with you, if you need the company."

Kris's eyes twinkled. "You're very kind, young man," he said. "But all I really need from both of you is a promise."

Chrissy looked at him skeptically.

"I want you both to always remember that home is not a place—it's a state of the heart."

Evan had pulled out his phone and was typing furiously in the Notes app. "Not ... a place ... state ... of ... heart. Wow," he said, looking up. "This is great stuff, man. Really brilliant. I have a friend who does amateur calligraphy on reclaimed slabs of wood, and she is going to *love* this."

Chrissy was still staring. "That's the most ridiculous thing I've ever heard," she said. "Are you really telling me you're just sadly hanging around outside, waiting for people to approach you, just so you can say inane platitudes like that?"

Kris laughed a big, booming laugh. As he laughed, his stomach shook, like ... hmm, Chrissy thought. Like a large container holding something edible. Like a bowl, she realized. It shook like a bowl full of ... pudding? Gelatin? Something viscous, that was for certain.

"Home *isn't* a state of the heart," Chrissy snapped, embarrassed by Kris's laughter. "Home is New York City."

"The Big Apple," Kris murmured to himself, reaching into a paper sack and removing a red delicious. "I'm so glad I saved this for my snack. Now, dear, I'm sorry, I completely missed what you were saying."

"Nothing," Chrissy said, lips pursed. "Don't worry about it. Ethan and I have to be on our way."

"Evan," whispered Evan.

"You know," Kris said, smiling at Chrissy. "We're not so different, you and I. Why do you think we practically share a name?"

Chrissy got into the car and slammed the door. She was agitated, and she didn't quite know why. Who did this Kris character think he was? Why were his eyes so twinkly? And his cheeks so rosy? Rosacea, Chrissy thought. Of course.

"Let's go home, Eric," she said at last.

He pulled away from the curb and began driving, and Kris became smaller and smaller in the rearview window. It was only once he was completely out of sight that a thought occurred to Chrissy: She had never introduced herself. She jolted upright.

How did Kris know her name?

Then, she heard a faint tinkling sound, like someone playing the world's tiniest bells.

"Did you hear that?" she asked Evan.

"Hear what?" Evan asked.

Chrissy sat back in her seat. "Never mind," she said. "Let's just drive."

Start reading at the *on page 45.*

Chrissy shook her head. "No," she said. "We already know everything we need to know about the guy. Comfy red and white clothing, black boots, white hair and beard, named Kris, classic regular, human, non-magical guy. I see nothing interesting coming of our pulling over, and I absolutely refuse to believe that there may be any symbolism here or that Kris is somehow the human embodiment of a lesson I've needed to learn for many, many years. I refuse to acknowledge the clues, which, to an outsider, may seem obvious, because I am angry, and I am from the city, and I'm going through business withdrawal. I haven't collated anything for a week, and honestly? I can't remember the last time I said, 'Per my last email.' So you'll excuse me if I'm a little out of sorts. Now for the last time," she concluded, "please just drive me home."

Start reading at the 🏠 *below.*

The car snaked through curvy back roads until it finally settled on a property just on the outskirts of town. Chrissy's childhood home. When she was younger, they'd lived in a small apartment closer to the center of town. At the time, they were growing candy canes on windowsills, on their balcony, in the small patch of grass in front of the building, wherever they could find. The peppermint business was brutal, and the candy cane sector was the most competitive of all—if Chrissy's family was ever going to build a sustainable business, they knew they were going to have to grind. So the small two-bedroom apartment had been overwhelmed by candy canes tucked into corners and behind the bathtub, sprouting out of little pots. But as her parents' candy cane farm grew and grew, things changed. They needed to expand the business and move to a place with a little more property.

"Your parents own a candy cane farm?" asked Evan, puzzled. "I thought those died out ages ago. Last I'd heard, candy canes were just … made from sugar and cornstarch and food dye and stuff."

Chrissy laughed. "Most candy canes are, these days. But Candy Cane Falls is a small town, and people do things the slow way here. So they may be old-fashioned, celebrating Christmas all month and growing their own candy canes, but—well, God love 'em, and I hate to admit it, but my parents were always right about one thing: They taste better than the store-bought stuff."

"Can there really be that much difference in the flavor of a candy cane?" Evan asked. "They seem pretty straightforward."

She laughed again. What a dumb boy she was dealing with. "Okay," she said, "here's what I want you to do: Close your eyes and imagine the flavor of a candy cane in your mouth. Are you imagining it?"

Evan closed his eyes. "Mm hmm," he said.

"Okay," she said, "now, imagine that flavor, but like, way better. Like *way* better. Now, open your eyes." Evan opened his eyes.

"Whoa," he said.

"Pretty amazing, right?" she asked. "That's the difference between homegrown and factory-made candy canes. Speaking of," she said, gesturing toward the house. "That's probably my cue to leave. Thanks for the ride. And if you're ever in the city and want someone to hustle and bustle with, look me up. I live in a harsh minimalist apartment that is primarily constructed of sharp corners. It's for women who don't want children. Anyway," she said, waving her hand, "I'm rambling. I must be going crazy from missing business so much. Thanks again for the ride. I had a nice time."

Then, she paused and looked back at him. She actually had had a nice time. She couldn't remember the last time she'd felt so relaxed. It was probably nothing, and she felt silly even thinking it, but did she … like this guy? They'd been cooped up inside his car for hours, and

not once—once!—had he made a joke about how, since they were stuck in his car, they were actually "couped" up, which for some reason was a pun Chrissy was certain he would make, one that would have been made worse by the fact that Evan's Prius wasn't even a coupe. It was unlikely, yes, but she had been hurt by men and their terrible puns before.

It wasn't just that, though; she also liked that he was nice. She talked easily with him. He kept his hands on the wheel at 10 and 2 the whole time, but not in a way where it seemed like he thought he was better than you, just where you knew it came naturally to him. And he was funny, too: After she had told him about a TED Talk she had recently heard (the power posing one, obviously), she asked him what—if he were absolutely forced to give a TED Talk—he would speak about. He paused for a moment, and then replied, "The origins and iterations of the name 'Theodore.'" It had taken until now, outside her home, for Chrissy to get the joke, and she laughed out loud. She appreciated the delayed gratification. It reminded her of her favorite TED Talk, the one about the Marshmallow Test.

And most importantly—for all the radio and podcasts they listened to during their drive—not once did Evan say, "You know, a couple of my buddies and I are actually thinking of starting a podcast." She literally had never met a man like him before.

Could this be fate? she wondered. Could this even be … love?

Should Chrissy …

 Try to go for it with Evan? *Turn to page 48 and start reading at the pine tree.*

 Say goodbye? *Turn to page 51 and start reading at the stars.*

"Wait," she said, taking her hand off the car door handle and turning to face him. "There's something I need to say."

Evan gripped and ungripped the steering wheel. Chrissy took a deep breath and looked him in the eyes. How did that saying in business go? "You have to spend money to make money." Maybe, she thought, in matters of the heart, you have to spend love to make love. Nope, do not say that out loud, she immediately thought in horror.

"This is going to sound ridiculous," she said at last, "but … do you want to run away together?"

> **"This is going to sound ridiculous, but … do you want to run away together?"**

"Yes," Evan said immediately, before she had even finished asking. "Yes! 100% yes."

He had actually initially answered "yes" when he thought she was asking, "Do you want to run?" because he was feeling a little cooped up and thought it would be nice to give his legs a stretch. But when he heard her full question, his heart leapt. He thought, maybe it's time I give … my heart a stretch. Nope, do not say that out loud, he immediately thought in horror. Then he thought, oh wait, more like COUPED up. Then he thought, ew, gross, also never say *that* out loud. Then, internally rolling his eyes, he realized that, since he drove a Prius sedan, the joke wouldn't even have worked on a basic level. Be better, Evan, he thought to himself angrily.

"Oh! I know!" he cried suddenly, reaching over to open his glove compartment. Something had just occurred to him. He fished around for a bit and finally found what he was looking for: a mistletoe-scented car freshener.

Chrissy cocked her head.

"Pine is more common," Evan explained, holding the miniature tree above their heads. "But I always thought the mistletoe scent might come in handy if I ever met—"

Chrissy kissed him before he had time to finish the sentence.

"Wanna get out of here?" Evan asked, revving the engine, which, as he drove a Prius, did not quite have the effect he was going for.

"Yeah," Chrissy said, smiling. "Let's go."

Evan backed the car out of the driveway and pulled back onto the road. Chrissy glanced up at the rearview mirror.

"Huh," she said, squinting. "I know that's my mom on the porch—she's the one waving her hands around yelling for us to come back. But I can't quite make out who's next to her. By his general shape and silhouette, I want to say it's … someone I knew in high school who over the years has grown, both physically and emotionally, into the man I deserve, if only we could both, over the course of the time we would have spent together in Candy Cane Falls, find a way to get over our differences and love each other?"

She stared into the mirror for a few seconds longer.

"Could also just be the mailman," she said.

Evan's car sped away down the long, country roads until Chrissy's house was just a speck on the horizon. She sat back against the passenger seat and sighed contentedly. It would be hours before it crossed her mind that maybe she could have just asked him out for coffee. Just, like, started small.

But she wasn't thinking that right now. Right now, she was watching the mistletoe air freshener swing from the rearview mirror and thinking that she was so happy that she could listen to a TED Talk about happiness. Maybe a Dan Gilbert one.

She grabbed Evan's hand and squeezed, and he squeezed back. Then, suddenly, they both fell silent: Somewhere just in the distance was the faint, delicate sound of tinkling bells. They turned toward each other and grinned.

"You hear that too, right?" asked Chrissy.

"Yeah," Evan said, and then stopped to listen a little harder. "Actually, it sounds like 'Christmas Eve/Sarajevo 12/24.'"

"That's actually my favorite Christmas song," they both said at the same time.

"Okay, worst Christmas song of all time," Chrissy said. "Go!"

"'Little Saint Nick' by the Beach Boys!" Evan said immediately.

"We know that Christmas comes this time each year!" Chrissy exclaimed. "That's, like, the one main, definite thing we know!"

"The Gregorian calendar has been around since Pope Gregory XIII introduced it in 1582, Brian Wilson!" Evan shouted. "We don't need a musical reminder as well!"

"Yeah, Brian Wilson," said Chrissy, laughing. "Did you think we would be confused because we're still, like, relying on the Julian calendar or something?"

"Sure, let's use the Julian calendar … said no one ever!" Evan cried, practically in tears from laughter.

"No one who cares about a little something called equinox drift, that is!" Chrissy giggled.

They spent the rest of the car drive talking about the history of calendars, the influence of the papacy, and why they suspected that Brian Wilson, a Californian, genius though he may be, might have just been "too warm" to write a good Christmas song.

It was, they would both think to themselves later, the best car ride either of them had ever been on.

And Evan had once won $4,200 in the Cash Cab.

The End

"He's not the love of your life," she whispered to herself. "He just isn't immediately interested in starting a podcast. And there is a difference."

"Thanks again," she said, smiling at Evan.

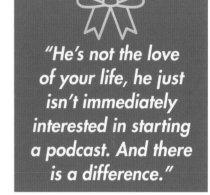

"Oh, wait!" he said. "*Hanks Again*! I totally forgot, but you just reminded me! This whole time, I've been meaning to tell you about this podcast I just started with a few of my buddies. It's called *Hanks Again*, and basically every week we just talk about sequels and prequels that Tom Hanks has done."

Chrissy thought for a second.

"So just the *Toy Story* and the *Da Vinci Code* movies?" she finally asked.

"He's not the love of your life, he just isn't immediately interested in starting a podcast. And there is a difference."

"No!" Evan shot back. "He also had a minor role in *The Rutles 2: Can't Buy Me Lunch*. But otherwise yes, that's it."

Chrissy smiled, suddenly exhausted.

"Maybe I will check it out," she said, stepping out of the car. "See ya."

"If you use the code HANKS4THEMEMORIES you can get 5 percent off your next mattress subscription box!" he called out the window.

"I don't know what that means!" she responded, waving as the car drove away. "Five stars!" she called, suddenly remembering the name of a Nativity-themed shop back in town. She'd been trying to think of it all day.

She didn't have time to think about that, though, because the screen door banged open and her mother rushed out to envelop her in a hug.

"Ugh," Chrissy grunted, smothered under the embrace. "It's nice … to see … you too." She finally wriggled free.

"Come inside," said her mom, smiling. "I have a surprise for you."

"A surprise?" asked Chrissy. "This close to Christmas?"

"Just come in," her mother said, grabbing her by the hand and practically dragging her across the front porch, through the foyer, and into the kitchen.

"As you know," her mother said, "the candy cane harvest was huge this year. Oh, here, Chrissy, will you hold these for me for a minute?" she asked, scooping a stack of recipe books off of the counter and into Chrissy's arms. Chrissy nodded and clumsily accepted the books.

"Anyway," her mother continued, "even though I try to avoid it, I knew that I was probably going to have to hire someone to help me with the winter rush."

Chrissy nodded again.

"And wouldn't you know," she continued, "but one day, I was out at the Christmas cookie store trying to place an order, and who should walk in but—"

"Me," said Nick. He had entered the kitchen through the backdoor when no one was paying attention.

"Nicholas Bell," Chrissy gasped, dropping all of the books to the floor.

Should Nick be …

 Chrissy's high school nemesis with whom she has always shared a weird chemistry? *Turn to page 53 and start reading at the caterpillar.*

 Chrissy's former high school flame? *Turn to page 57 and start reading at the bell.*

"Well, well, well," said Nick. He was looking just beyond Chrissy to the wall, where there was a painting of three wishing wells. He studied the painting for a moment more, and then turned his attention back to Chrissy.

"Chrissy," he said, "What a surprise. I didn't know the convention was in town."

"What convention?" asked Chrissy, confused.

"You know," Nick said, a smile spreading over his face, "the Caterpillar Reading Group convention."

Chrissy felt her face go red with anger.

"I wouldn't know," Nick continued, "because, as you know, I myself was in the Butterfly Reading Group."

"That. was. fourth. grade," Chrissy hissed. "After all these years, I can't believe you're still bringing this up! And besides, I belonged in the Butterfly Group, but, as everyone knows, my Accelerated Reader test results were sabotaged."

"You're still sticking to that story, huh?" asked Nick. "Remind me again, who sabotaged you? Was it Ms. Bukworhm, the sweet old librarian?"

"She was the only one with access to the machines!" Chrissy cried. "And she had motive! She knew that if anyone found out how high my actual reading ability was, pretty soon, I wouldn't be satisfied with *Super Fudge* or *Freckle Juice*; she knew I was going to start asking for the other Blumes, the Blumes that made parents call the library and yell at her! She knew I was going to ask her for *Forever*, and she knew that if she could just keep me in the lower reading group for the rest of the school year, then she could retire and I would be the next librarian's problem!"

Nick shrugged. "I mean, it sounds like you've really thought about this a lot," he said. "I remember being surprised that you were still upset about it in high school, but I guess I always assumed that that was because you were self-conscious about how I was valedictorian, when you were just the lowly salutatorian. I guess I just assumed you would have moved on by now. I mean, I certainly have."

"First of all," Chrissy snapped, "you know that the only reason you were valedictorian is because I took honors classes and they didn't weigh the grades, while you, Mr. All-Star Athlete, got to take classes like 'Math for Athletes' and 'Special Topics in History for Athletes: 1980 Olympics Only' and 'Sitting and Playing Games in Your TI-83 Calculator in Coach Piron's Room During His Prep Period Because He Was the Football Coach and Somehow Had That Power 101.'"

"Math for Athletes was tough," Nick admitted. "I still remember on our final how we had to use everything we'd learned in class to figure out how many basketball hoops are on a basketball court."

Chrissy muttered something.

"What did you say?" Nick asked, grinning. "I couldn't hear you."

"I said," Chrissy repeated, more loudly, "spoken like a true Matt Christopher."

Nick flushed.

"Ah," Chrissy said. Now she was the one who was smiling. "I guess you do remember your nickname. So you must remember how even though you were in the top reading group, it was only because you exclusively read those Matt Christopher sports books. And they artificially inflated your score. And everybody knew."

Nick stared at her for a few seconds, blinking.

"*The Dog That Pitched a No-Hitter* was a classic," he said, finally, "and you know that. And besides," he shrugged, "I don't even think about our old rivalry stuff anymore. I'm a really happy, successful adult. I have a son, actually."

"I have an incredible business job," Chrissy retorted. *Had* a business job, she silently corrected herself. But Nick didn't need to know that.

"I've had tons of girlfriends," Nick continued.

BUILD YOUR OWN CHRISTMAS MOVIE ROMANCE

"Oh yeah," said Chrissy, "I've been married a *bunch* of times. Like, a bunch." She winced. Not only was that not true, but it also didn't quite come across as the brag she meant it to.

Nick took a small step toward her.

"I've grown really deep roots in Candy Cane Falls," he said, "and while it may not have everything a big city does, it has something more important: community. I love knowing that I'm investing in a tight-knit community that invests right back in me. And did you know that the tire swing my son swings on is tied to a tree upon whose trunk my great-grandparents carved their initials when they were courting? My life is truly beautiful. Because I have love."

"And I," responded Chrissy proudly, "have a Peloton."

Without realizing it, she had also taken a small step toward Nick. Now they were just inches apart, both staring at the other. A few moments passed in silence. Then Nick rolled up the sleeves of his flannel shirt, revealing his veiny forearms. Chrissy seethed. This was a dirty tactic. He must have known that she had a weakness for veiny forearms. They're the only attractive veins! It was a truth universally acknowledged. Chrissy closed her eyes. Snap out of this, she thought.

"I thought at first that maybe this was going to be a group conversation. I now understand that it was not."

"This has been great," she finally said, "but I'm going to go and find my mom now."

"I've actually been here this whole time," said a small voice from behind her. Chrissy spun around, and practically bumped right into her mother, who had been standing behind her the entire time.

"I thought at first that maybe this was going to be a group conversation," her mom continued. "I now understand that it was not."

Chrissy started to say something, but Nick cut in instead.

"Actually," he said, "I should get back to work. Those candy canes won't harvest themselves." He winked at Chrissy's mom, who blushed.

"Oh, Nick," she said, blushing and waving her hand as she left the room. "You're too much."

Nick turned back to Chrissy and stuck out his hand.

"Nice to see my favorite salutatorian," he said. "It's been too long."

Chrissy reached out and grabbed his hand. She tried for a clever comeback, but all that came out was, "Smart ... sports."

Nick cocked an eyebrow. For a moment, it seemed like he was going to tease her, but he decided against it.

Finally, he leaned in close to whisper something to her. He was still holding her hand.

"*Forever* is good," he breathed into her ear, "but when it comes to Blume, I always preferred *Deenie*." Then he gave her hand a hard shake, let go, and walked out the back door.

Chrissy stood frozen in that spot in the kitchen for minutes after Nick left. She might have stayed there all night, had her mother not bustled back through, noticed her, and said, "Chrissy! What are you still doing in the kitchen? Can I get you something to eat?"

Chrissy shook her head slowly.

"No," she said slowly, "thank you."

But what she was thinking was that until today, she'd always thought she was the only person in the world who preferred *Deenie*.

Start reading at the *on page 57.*

"Wow," said Nick. "If it isn't Chrissy Kristen Christopher," he added, dropping to his knee to scoop up the recipe books, all while grinning his famous humble, non-threatening, deeply attractive grin that felt like putting on a warm hoodie, or sinking into a soft couch, or peeling the plastic off a brand-new phone. In the high school yearbook, he had actually been voted Most Likely to Have a Humble, Non-Threatening, Deeply Attractive Grin That Felt Like Putting On a Warm Hoodie, or Sinking Into a Soft Couch, or Peeling the Plastic Off a Brand-New Phone, although of course, the caption got cut off because of space limitations. "How long has it been? Probably since—"

"—since Senior Prom. You were wearing that light blue tux that accentuated your forearm veins, and—"

"—and you were stunning in that sparkling ..."

" ... spaghetti-strap silver dress," they finished the thought together.

"Jinx!" they both shouted. "Double jinx! You owe me a coke!" They were still shouting in rhythm. "Diet Coke! Coke Zero! Sprite!" Still, they continued on as if in one voice. "Store-brand Dr. Pepper! Actual Dr. Pepper! Mr. Pibb if Dr. Pepper isn't available! Mellow Yellow! Surge! Oh man, remember Surge?"

Finally, they both doubled over, out of breath.

"We know so many soda brands and flavors," gasped Chrissy.

"We really do," said Nick, breathing deeply.

Chrissy's mom gaped.

"Anyway," Nick said, "it was a beautiful dress."

"Well," she said blushing, "my hairdo certainly left something to be desired." Suddenly, she didn't know what to do with her hands. What does one do with one's hands while one is talking? she wondered. She placed them both on her belly. No, that wasn't right. One flat on the countertop, the other with the palm facing up? Close, but also wrong. She finally decided to just stick them in her pockets, but when she tried, she realized that her jeans had false pockets that didn't open at all, so she thought some angry thoughts about feminism and the clothing industry, and awkwardly just rested her hands on her upper thighs.

"Well, Nick," she said, finally. "I have to go unpack, but I guess I'll be seeing you around."

"I guess you will," he said.

Chrissy walked out of the kitchen toward the stairs. She stopped to glance back at Nick, who was looking out the back window. She smiled and started up the stairs to her room. Nick glanced away from the window and watched her. He smiled and shook his head. Chrissy took a few more steps and then looked back again, but by this point, she was already in her room and only saw the closed door. "Darn," she thought. She was very good at business, but she was not very smart in love. Or spatial awareness.

SCENE 4

THE WINTERY FROLIC

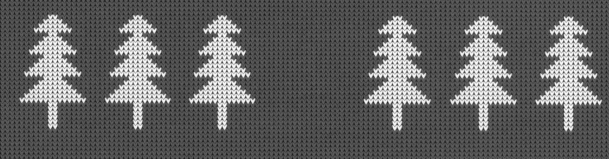

It took Chrissy hours to fall asleep that night. She tossed and turned, thinking about Nick, thinking about thinking about Nick, thinking about how much she wanted to not be thinking about Nick. Think about something else, she told herself. Something boring. So she tried to think about things that bored her: people who think that it's interesting to hate pumpkin spice, people who like to argue about whether hot dogs are sandwiches, people who use the word "sportsball," people who still make jokes about Nickelback, the music of Nickelback, live baseball games once she's finished eating her hot dog, the movie *Fantasia* … None of it worked, in part because she forgot that *Fantasia* was, along with being boring, also kind of scary.

She tried to trick herself into falling asleep by counting backward from Nick, but that presented more troubles than it solved.

And when she finally fell asleep, do you know what she dreamed about? Her teeth falling out. But then later, also about Nick. Nick chopping down a Christmas tree. Nick wrapping presents. Nick drinking hot cocoa. Nick saying, "In my family, we got to open one present on Christmas Eve. It was usually pajamas." Really, the entire night just a dreamscape of Nick in a Christmas activity montage.

Are Nick and Chrissy ...

 Did you choose for Nick and Chrissy to be rivals? *Turn to page 62 and start reading at the reindeer.*

 Did you choose for Nick and Chrissy to be high school sweethearts? *Turn to page 63 and start reading at the candle.*

When she woke up the next morning, she was still, unbelievably, frustratingly, thinking about Nick. What did he think he was doing, showing up at her house like this? High school had been bad enough, the two of them constantly competing at everything and Nick almost always coming out on top. A fact about which he'd be the first to remind you, Chrissy thought, rolling her eyes. In fact, he had reminded everyone in his valedictorian speech. How had his opening lines gone? Something like: "Welcome to graduation, Candy Cane Falls High School Fightin' Reindeer! My name is Nick, and I am thrilled and honored to be delivering the graduation address this evening. Not as thrilled as, I'm sure, Chrissy Christopher would have been, but thrilled nonetheless. Moving on. Webster's Dictionary defines 'school' as …"

She couldn't stand the guy. He was so cocky, so arrogant, so—she clenched her firsts— infuriatingly right about Judy Blume books.

Stop thinking about him, she told herself for the tenth time. He's so vain, he would be thrilled to know that she'd lost sleep over him. He's so, so vain.

So, so, so (her mind drifted once more back to his forearm) vein.

Start reading at the *on page 63.*

The next morning, she felt confused. Usually she considered her Christmas dreams nightmares, but these were … different. Nice, even. Wouldn't that make her mother happy, she smirked to herself. Marrying a boy from Candy Cane Falls and never returning to the big city again. Well, she thought, that will never happen. After all her years in the city, she knew that she could only fall in love with someone who spoke in a brusque tone, and say all you will about Nick's abs—no, really, please do—but he spoke gently and at a normal pace and volume. This would just not do for a businesswoman from the city like Chrissy. I never get tired of limiting myself like this, she thought sleepily, and then drifted back to sleep.

Start reading at the *below.*

When she finally came downstairs later that morning, Nick was already out back, hard at work in the candy cane fields.

"Here, honey," said her mother, bustling about the kitchen. "I made you some morning candy cane hot chocolate."

Chrissy clasped the mug in two hands and took a deep breath through the rising steam.

"What strain of mint is this, Mom?" she asked.

"I thought you would notice," her mom replied. "That's from this year's candy cane harvest. We're calling it Noel Limits. Your dad would have been really proud of this one."

> **"Please—I was a teenager in the '60s. I've forgotten more strains of peppermint than you'll ever try."**

"It's so minty, but it's still really smooth," said Chrissy, ignoring the comment about her father. It was too painful. "I can feel it tingling through my entire body."

Her mother nodded. "Yes, Noel Limits is definitely a body peppermint, as opposed to the other little crop we tried out this year, Christmas Blaze. That one you feel more in your head."

"This really is like medical-grade mintiness, Mom," Chrissy said, impressed. "I didn't think this was your style. I'm actually kind of surprised you can handle this."

Her mom rolled her eyes. "Please," she said. "I was a teenager in the '60s. I've forgotten more strains of peppermint than you'll ever try."

"It's really delicious, Mom," Chrissy said, savoring the candy.

Her mother beamed with pride. "I was really pleased with this year's crop. I guess there must have just been a little extra Christmas magic around the house this year."

And like that, Chrissy's good mood disappeared. "There's no such thing as magic, Mom," she said. "And there's no such thing as Christmas."

"Well that second part is just patently untrue," her mother said. "It's a bank holiday."

Chrissy's face clouded. "You know what I mean. You always do this. You always have to bring up Christmas."

"Well, it's really hard not to—" her mom started, when Chrissy interrupted.

"This kind of conversation would *never* happen in the big city," she snapped.

A furious silence hung between them.

"I think I'll go see if Nick wants any hot chocolate," Chrissy said finally. "Since the harvest is so big, I mean," she added quickly. "Since it's such a big, strong harvest. I just want to make sure he has energy to harvest. I'm doing this for you, Mom," she concluded, unconvincingly.

"Good idea," her mother said quietly.

"I'm … sorry, "Chrissy said. "I shouldn't have yelled. You know how hard it's been since the incident."

"I know, Honey," her mom replied. "But that was years ago. You've got to move on. Or you've at least got to be able to have an in-depth conversation with me about it right here and right now."

Should Chrissy ...

 Continue the conversation about "the incident" with her mom? *Start reading at the cabin below.*

 Ignore her and move on to the next subject? *Turn to page 73 and start reading at the bell.*

"Fine, Mom," Chrissy snapped. "You want to talk about it? Let's talk about it."

Her mother's eyes widened, as though she hadn't expected the conversation to go in this direction.

"I didn't expect this conversation to go in this direction," she said.

"I know," said Chrissy. "I can tell by how your eyes widened."

"Okay," her mom sighed. "Let's get down to business."

Chrissy perked up. Then she realized: Oh, right. Not that kind of business.

"All I know," her mother continued, "is that before ten years ago, you loved Christmas. And then we took that Christmas trip to the cabin, and ever since, I've hardly been able to mention Christmas in your presence. And then you moved to the city, and your shoulders and elbows got sharper, it seemed, and since then you've just been … different," she finished. "A briefcase in the shape of a woman, if I could be so bold."

"Do you remember, Mom, what happened that weekend in the cabin?" Chrissy asked.

"Oh, sure," her mother replied. "That was an eventful one. I remember we were locked out when we arrived, even though we'd let the Airbnb host know that we'd be there at six, and I remember how the first night, I spilled my hot chocolate and said, 'Clumsy much?!' and everyone laughed, which made me feel good, so I said it again, only you guys didn't laugh as hard the second time, and I remember how difficult the shower faucet was to work—"

"You had to push in and *then* turn," Chrissy interrupted.

"Exactly," her mom said. "And I remember those carolers came by and sang to all of us, and then one by one they all tramped back out into the snow, except the one little boy who stayed behind, the one who was using a cane and wearing one of those old-timey newsboy caps and jangling a tin cup. And I remember he asked for you specifically, by name, and his eyes got all sparkly, and he said something that seemed very ominous, you remember," her mother leaned in and whispered the mysterious phrase to Chrissy. "And then," she continued, "there was the sound of quietly tinkling bells in the air, and the little boy kind of vanished into the mist, and then afterward we wanted to make dinner and we absolutely could *not* find where they stored the colanders, but then we finally found them in the lower-left cabinets, but that's when we remembered we were eating pizza, but we'd spent all that time looking that we didn't want it to have been a waste, so then we shoved the pizza through the colander holes anyway, and then I went to the bathroom, and when I came back your father had died, and then we figured out that the reason we'd been having so much trouble with the Wi-Fi was that the password had the number one in it, not an *i*, and then basically that was the weekend."

"Do you remember," Chrissy said slowly, "the part of the story where you said you went to the bathroom?"

"Of course," her mother replied.

"And do you remember what happened right after you went to the bathroom?" Chrissy asked.

"Sure," her mom said, "we started looking for the colander."

"That's not—" Chrissy started.

"Your father died," her mother interrupted. "Of course I knew that was what you were referring to. Considering the tone of this conversation, and the weighing of significance between events, it would be absolutely absurd for me to assume that what you were referring to was not the tragic death of your father, but instead an adjacent, but absolutely banal activity."

Chrissy nodded, her eyes full of tears.

"What I never told you," she said, her voice quavering, "was that when Dad died that night … it was my fault."

"What do you mean?" her mother asked, concerned. She hated secrets.

"Well, you know what the paramedics said was his cause of death," Chrissy said.

Her mother nodded. "Yes," she said, reminiscing. "I think the exact quote was, 'Well, guess his sleigh just ran out of gas.'"

"Yes," said Chrissy. "It was extremely folksy. It also completely obscured the fact that he died from a snakebite, and … also demonstrated a fundamental misunderstanding of how sleighs work."

"It was kind of cute how they decorated the inside of the ambulance with holly wreaths for Christmas," her mom admitted.

"I remember that," Chrissy smiled. "I can still picture it: the holly … and the I.V."

"Sure," her mom said. "But I know all of this. I went to the bathroom, and when I came back, I found out your father had been bitten by a grinch snake, the only venomous snake active during Christmas break in the midwestern United States."

"But what you don't know," Chrissy said, sniffling, "is that I tried to save him, and I … I messed it all up. I failed. And now, it's my fault he's dead, and I'll never celebrate another Christmas as long as I live." She buried her head in her hands.

"Of course it's not your fault," her mother said, rubbing Chrissy's back, although she was, of course, curious to hear more. Because maybe it was Chrissy's fault? A little bit?

"It is," Chrissy sobbed. "It is. Because as soon as I saw that Dad had been bitten, I did what you always taught me to do in the case of a freak winter snakebite: I melted down a quart of candy canes and then I spread the resulting peppermint goo over his wound like a salve."

"You did everything right, Sweetie," her mom cooed. "Everything. Everyone knows that a viscous glop of melted candy cane is the first, best, and only treatment for an unexpected winter grinch snake bite."

> *"Everyone knows that a viscous glop of melted candy cane is the first, best, and only treatment for an unexpected winter grinch snake bite."*

"I know you've always said that," Chrissy said. "But I couldn't make it work. The simplest cure in the world, and I botched it. And that's how I know it's my fault."

Her mom sighed.

"Honey," she said, slowly, "there's something you should know. Something your dad and I tried to hide from you. Now I realize we never should have."

"What is it?" asked Chrissy. Was her dad secretly a king? she wondered to herself.

"Before your dad, who was not a king, died," her mother explained, "we had been going through a rough patch, financially. The business was losing money, fast. We tried everything we could, but it soon became clear that we were going to lose the whole candy cane business if we didn't take drastic measures. And so we did what we swore we'd never do." She paused and took a deep breath. Then, looking Chrissy in the eyes, she said, "We started using genetically modified ingredients in our candy canes."

Chrissy gasped. "Like from that evil corporation Monsanta?" she asked. "I thought you were completely against them."

"We were," her mom reassured. "We *are*. But for a time, that was the only way we could cut costs until we were profitable again. We were so ashamed, but we didn't know what else to do."

"Okay," Chrissy said. "But I guess I don't see what that has to do with the night Dad died."

Chrissy's mom brushed her hair back from her face.

"Don't you see, Sweetie?" she asked. "Those candy canes you used to try to make the salve … you didn't know it, but they were the genetically modified ones. They don't have the same healing properties that naturally grown candy canes do. We should have told you about the Monsanta deal from the beginning. You did everything right, but there was nothing you could have done that night. It was never your fault."

Chrissy sat down hard in a chair, a wave of relief washing over her. It *hadn't* been her fault. She still had one more question, though.

"I still spent a good twenty minutes making the salve before calling the paramedics," she admitted. "I never considered it before, but do … do you think maybe I should have called sooner?"

Chrissy's mother gripped her by the shoulders. "Now listen here, young lady. There is not a person alive on this Earth who wouldn't have made the exact same choice as you. What could a paramedic do that a glob of melted candy can't?"

"Fall in love," Chrissy answered.

"But medically," her mom continued. "Why would you ever choose a paramedic over a candy cane?"

Chrissy shrugged and looked at the floor. Maybe her mother was right. Maybe her father's death hadn't been her fault after all. Maybe … maybe now she could stop hating Christmas?

Just then, there was that same faint tinkling sound again, like bells.

"You hear that, right?" Chrissy asked.

"Hmm?" her mom replied absently. "Hear what?"

"Nothing," Chrissy muttered.

Are Nick and Chrissy ...

 Did you choose for Nick and Chrissy to be rivals? *Start reading at the apple below.*

 Did you choose for Nick and Chrissy to be high school sweethearts? *Turn to page 72 and start reading at the football.*

Movement outside the window caught Chrissy's attention. "What's Ned doing out there, anyway?" she asked, in a purposefully casual tone.

Her mom gave her a look.

"You mean Nick?" she asked.

"Oh, right, whatever," said Chrissy, flipping her hair. "Nick. I think about him so little, I'm always forgetting. So what's what's-his-name doing out wherever? Don't answer, I don't actually care." She paused. "You can answer if you want."

"He's harvesting candy canes," her mother responded. "He had a few weeks off of work for the holiday, and when he heard I needed help, he was the first to volunteer."

"That doesn't sound like the Nick I know," said Chrissy. "I mean Ned. Whoever. I slept well last night. What kind of job just gives you a few weeks off in December? What is he, CEO of ... Not Working?"

"He's an award-winning first-grade teacher," her mom said.

Chrissy found her mouth had gone dry.

"Probably just wanted to relive the glory days," she said. "Forget not being able to leave high school behind: He couldn't even leave elementary school behind. Pretty sad."

"Well, he's not teaching at your elementary school," her mom corrected her.

Chrissy furrowed her brow. How was that possible? There was only one elementary school in town.

"He's actually teaching at the children's hospital," her mother explained.

Chrissy's mouth had gone dry.

"On a special unit for children who are terminally cute," her mom continued. "They'll be okay, medically," she added quickly. "It's just that their cuteness is very advanced."

Chrissy's eyes were having a hard time focusing.

"Nick's co-teacher is a golden retriever," her mom said after a moment. "That felt important to add."

Chrissy shook her head. "That doesn't make sense," she said. "I know Nick. He's the most self-absorbed person I've ever met."

"Have you ever considered," her mother started, "that maybe Nick is a different person than he was in high school?"

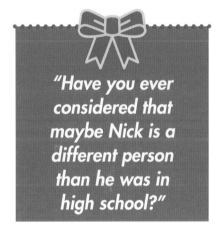

"Have you ever considered that maybe Nick is a different person than he was in high school?"

Chrissy shrugged.

"You've certainly changed since you were in school," her mom added. "Remember back when *Jurassic Park* came out, how you had that gigantic crush on Jeff Goldblum? And now that you're an adult, I'm sure the very idea feels silly to you."

"Right," said Chrissy slowly. "It's definitely not a crush that has miraculously improved with age and grows stronger every day."

"Exactly," said her mom. "You've changed. It's the same with Nick."

"You think I should bring him that hot chocolate?" Chrissy finally asked.

Her mom grinned slyly. "You could," she said.

"Okay," Chrissy nodded. "I will."

But as she walked out the back door and into the candy cane fields, it occurred to Chrissy for the first time: When it came to bringing Nick hot chocolate, she had been so preoccupied with whether she could, she didn't stop to think about if she should.

Start reading at the (🍬) *on page 74.*

"I guess I should go see if Nick needs anything," Chrissy said at last.

"Well, I'm *sure* he would enjoy that," her mother said, a slow smile spreading over her face.

"Mo-o-m," Chrissy whined. "It's not like that. It's chilly, and he's been working hard, and I simply thought I should bring him some candy cane hot chocolate."

"That's very thoughtful," her mom replied, still grinning.

"It's not thoughtful," Chrissy snapped. "It's medically necessary. When Nick was in high school and playing football, sometimes he'd get so sweaty and exhausted during a game that he'd practically pass out. It was always up to me to revive him, so I'd grab a bottle of Gatorade ..."

"... and then dump out that bottle and fill it to the brim with candy cane hot chocolate," her mom finished. "I remember."

"When you work that hard for that long, your body starts sweating out all of your stores of candy cane hot chocolate," Chrissy said. "So you have to replenish it."

"I sure do miss watching Nick out on that football field," her mother sighed, reminiscing. "Do you remember the championship your junior year?"

"How could I forget?" Chrissy said. "They won in overtime, and the team was so excited that they dumped that gigantic orange cooler of hot chocolate all over Coach Morris."

"He was so horribly burned," her mom smiled.

"It was so graphic that one of the attending physicians passed out," Chrissy remembered. She paused again, smiling. Reminiscing. Then, with a start, she came back to the present. "I'm going to bring him a mug," she declared. "And that's all I'm doing."

Start reading at the *on page 74.*

"You know I can't, Mom," Chrissy said. Just then, there was that same faint tinkling, like bells.

"You hear that, right?" Chrissy asked.

"Hmm? Hear what?" her mother replied absently.

"Nothing," Chrissy muttered. In the city, they played popular rock music at cool unknown venues everyone knew about. In Candy Cane Falls, your brain tricked you into hearing fairy music that no one else noticed. *Another checkmark in favor of the city*, Chrissy thought, rolling her eyes.

"You should get outside and see Nick," her mom said, winking.

"Mom! Stop," Chrissy whined. "I'm just being polite. Everyone knows that after a lot of hard, sweaty manual labor, the best thing for you is a mug full of thick hot chocolate milk."

"That is what the town nutritionist always said," her mom acknowledged. "May he rest in peace."

"May he rest in peace," Chrissy repeated.

Start reading at the *below.*

She marched out to the candy cane fields until she found Nick at last, plucking candy canes from the ground and tossing them into a large, festive bucket. People from the big city might not know this, but when candy canes come out of the ground they're uncut—instead of having a hook on just one end, there is a hook on each end. After harvesting, one of the hooks is chopped off, leaving the J-shaped candy people know and love.

"Nick," she said, but he didn't respond.

"*Nick*," she said a little louder. Still nothing.

"*Nick*!" she shouted this time, and that got his attention. He turned around.

Are Nick and Chrissy ...

 Did you choose for Nick and Chrissy to be rivals? *Turn to page 75 and start reading at the bee.*

 Did you choose for Nick and Chrissy to be high school sweethearts? *Turn to page 77 and start reading at the dog.*

BUILD YOUR OWN CHRISTMAS MOVIE ROMANCE

"Sorry!" he called, looking up at last. "I was just thinking about, uh, just thinking about … "

He paused.

"I was thinking," he continued at last, "about that time at the ninth grade spelling bee when it came down to the both of us, and you went out on 'humuhumunukunukuāapua'a.' Pretty amateur move."

Chrissy felt her face start to flush.

"I spelled it correctly," she snapped. "I knew there was a kahakō over the antepenultimate 'a.' I just didn't know I was expected to tell that to the judges. And anyway, didn't Coach Piron read all of your clues to you? What word did you win on again?"

"I believe it was 'numb,'" Nick said, grinning widely. "Coach was very proud of me for getting the silent 'b.'"

"You know what—" Chrissy started, but then Nick held up his hand, stopping her.

"No, wait, wait, wait," he said. "You're right."

"I … am?" Chrissy asked, confused. "You actually think I'm right about the spelling bee?"

Nick rolled his eyes.

"Not just the spelling bee," he said, "All of it. You think I don't know who the best speller at the bee was? You think I don't know who actually deserved to be valedictorian? Come on, Chrissy. I know I'm not as smart as you, but I'm not dumb. I knew it, you knew it, everyone always knew it." He shrugged. "I guess I acted the way I did back then because I was just embarrassed to be …" He trailed off for a second. "Just embarrassed to be the biggest dumb-dumb in the world, I guess," he said quietly.

"Hey," Chrissy said interjecting. "Absolutely not. You drive me nuts, but I won't let you talk about yourself that way. You *aren't* the biggest dumb-dumb in the world. You're actually very—"

Nick burst out laughing, cutting her off.

"No, stop, stop, don't do this," he said, still laughing. "I was kidding. I'm sorry. Come on, I know I'm not the biggest dumb-dumb in the world, Chrissy. I'm definitely not as smart as you—" Hearing this admission, Chrissy blushed so hard she matched the red stripes on the candy canes."

> *"I don't mean to brag, but I read all of Bridge to Terabithia during silent reading time. I never even told anyone."*

"But I'm perfectly average. Like, I may have ridden the Matt Christopher train into the Butterfly Reading Group, but once I was there, I held my own. I don't mean to brag," he shrugged. "But I read all of *Bridge to Terabithia* during silent reading time. I never even told anyone."

"But that's a sixth-grade book," Chrissy said. "And besides, how did you get through that book without crying? I think I would have noticed."

"You don't remember when I was suddenly diagnosed with allergies that year?" Nick asked.

"Sure," Chrissy said, slowly, remembering.

"Well, it turns out, I wasn't allergic to pollen," Nick said. "I was allergic to a little chapter called 'No!'"

Chrissy clapped her hands over her mouth.

"The watercolor paint set floating down the river," she whispered.

Nick bit his lip. "The way his father does the milking for him that morning," he whispered back. "That was what got me."

"Exactly—no, wait a minute," Chrissy said, suddenly snapping out of her *Terabithia* trance. "What are you doing? Why are you telling me all of this now?" Chrissy asked.

"Because after last night, I couldn't stop thinking about how I didn't want you to think that I was still the arrogant jerk you knew in high school," Nick shrugged. "We probably won't become best friends, but if we're going to be stuck with each other for the next few weeks, I thought maybe it would be nice to maybe ... start fresh? Maybe be friends?"

Chrissy eyed him suspiciously.

"You never wanted to be friends," she said. "You were too busy trying to make my life miserable."

"Maybe I liked you and just didn't know how to express it!" Nick cried.

"The idea that young boys, like, pull pigtails and call girls names because they have crushes on them is actually super toxic!" Chrissy exclaimed.

"That actually makes a lot of sense!" Nick shouted back. "And it will affect how I teach my son to treat women! But come on, Chrissy, why do you think I did the spelling bee and all that other stuff if it wasn't to try to spend time with you?"

Start reading at the *on page 79.*

"Sorry," Nick said, sheepishly. "I was just lost in thought about how much I love rescue dogs. Then I got distracted by thinking about how to be a good father to my son, since I'm a single dad. Then I got distracted from that by thinking about whether six abs are enough, or if I should push myself for eight. I don't want to be vain, but physical health is so important to me since my grandfather perished in a tragic accident of not having enough abs. He was my best friend, and every night, I sing the folk melodies he sang to me as a child to my own son. Then I cry, because I'm not afraid to, and because tenderness is beauty, and beauty is strength, and strength is abs."

Chrissy took a step toward him, but he continued.

"And even if I hadn't been thinking about all of that," he said, "I would have been distracted by the language lessons I was listening to. I'm trying to learn Romanian, because I once saw a film that starred a Romanian actress who I so admired that I vowed then and there that I would learn Romanian in the off chance I ever met her, so that I could tell her how much her art meant to me, how much I respected her, and how much I knew that she, a woman in her eighties, could teach me. And then I would sit quietly at her feet and learn. That is," he clarified, "if she wanted. If not, I would simply say, 'Mulțumesc'—that's Romanian for thank you, as I'm sure you know—and go home forever changed."

Chrissy tried to say something, but Nick wasn't done.

"And of course, being around all these candy canes just makes you think," he said. "You know? About how open communication and trust are so important in a relationship, and how I hope that if I ever get married again, that it's to my best friend, and that every Christmas we'll buy matching pajama sets and take photos in front of the fire, and everyone who saw the pictures would think, 'You know, usually I find these photos cloying and obnoxious, proof positive that the spark has left the relationship, but somehow, with these two, it makes me believe that love is real and alive and that as they age, their relationship will only become steamier.' And I'll say, 'And doesn't that reindeer print bring out my wife's beautiful eyes?' And they'll be shocked to admit it, but they'll agree that somehow it does, and then later, when I quit social media to spend more time with orphans, everyone will mourn that they no longer can look at that photo, because it made them feel things they haven't felt since the first time they fell in love. Anyway," he sighed, "I was just thinking about all of that, so I didn't hear you come up. So what's up, Chrissy?"

Start reading at the on page 79.

Chrissy tried to respond, but no words came out. She opened her mouth over and over again, but no: just silence. She stood there croaking like a very emotionally overwhelmed frog, when finally she got one word to come tumbling out.

"*Hot,*" she croaked.

Nick raised his eyebrows.

"*Hot,*" she croaked again, trying to force out another word. Finally it came. "*Hot … chocolate.* Hot chocolate. Here," she said, thrusting the mug toward him. "I came here to say that I brought you candy cane hot chocolate. You looked like you were getting sweaty, so I thought I'd get you some—"

"—thick hot milk," he finished, smiling. "You remembered my favorite after-basketball snack!"

Oh yeah, thought Chrissy. I almost forgot he played every sport.

"How could I forget?" asked Chrissy. "I remember watching you at halftime, while all your teammates were sipping on Gatorades and waters, there you were, chugging a mug of steaming hot chocolate milk. You were … different from the other guys."

"And then I'd puke everywhere," he said, grinning.

"And then you'd puke everywhere," she agreed. "The janitors must have hated you."

"Actually, I'd usually stick around and help clean," Nick admitted. "School janitors are criminally overworked and underpaid, and I was obviously committing to a fluid regimen that was really pretty risky, puke-wise. Anyway," Nick said, accepting the mug at last and taking a long gulp. "Thank you. This is," he said, looking her deeply in the eyes, "exactly what I needed."

Chrissy started to blush when suddenly, she felt something wet land on her nose. She glanced up. It was starting to snow.

"Hey," she said, dumbly. "It's snowing."

"I've got an idea," said Nick. "I need to get these two rows harvested before this snow covers everything up. Let's make a game of it. You in?"

Chrissy nodded, still sorting through everything Nick had said in the last ten minutes.

"Take this," Nick said, handing her a bucket. "And we'll race. First one to finish their row wins. Ready?"

Chrissy nodded. She was doing so much nodding lately.

"On your mark, get set, go!" Nick cried, and immediately dropped to the ground, ripping candy canes out of the earth and throwing them into his bucket. At times, his arms seemed to be moving so fast that they were blurry, but then Chrissy realized she just had a snowflake in her eye.

"You're falling behind!" Nick called gleefully, as he moved down his row. Chrissy was still crouched at the very beginning of her row, struggling to yank a particularly stubborn candy cane out of the ground.

> *The candy cane popped out of the soil, sending Chrissy tumbling backward ... right into Nick, knocking him over.*

Not two minutes later, Chrissy heard Nick exclaim, "And … done!" He trotted back down the rows to Chrissy, pumping his fists in mock celebration.

"And meanwhile, I'm here still working on this first candy cane," Chrissy laughed. She gave it a tug. It was still stuck.

"Really plant your feet," Nick said from behind her. "Use your body weight to pull."

Chrissy dug her heels in, grasped the stubborn candy cane with both hands, and yanked. This time, it worked: The candy cane popped out of the soil, sending Chrissy tumbling backward ... right into Nick, knocking him over. He fell to the ground, and she landed on top of him.

Embarrassed, Chrissy tried to untangle herself from Nick and get up, but her efforts only made things worse: Somehow, she ended up belly to belly, nose to nose with Nick. She was close enough to smell his breath. It was minty.

Should Chrissy ...

 Apologize and get up? *Start reading at the mitten below.*

 Try to kiss him? *Turn to page 82 and start reading at the wreath.*

"Sorry," Chrissy whispered.

"Hey," he said, smiling. "What's red and white and dead all over?"

"What?" she said.

"Print media" he said soberly, poking her in the cheek where melted candy cane had left a festive stain. "I'm having a lot of fun with you right now, but even in times like these, I just think it's so important to remember the importance of high-quality local journalism."

"Yes, absolutely," she said, scrambling to get up. Local news was so important. In fact, back when she first moved to the city, she used to subscribe to a small, local paper. What was it called again? *The New York ... Gazette? The New York ... Situations? The Big City Times?* Odd, she thought. She had never forgotten something about living in the city before. She quizzed herself nightly regarding all the details of her business and city life, just in case anyone from a small town ever challenged her about anything, ever. But now ... was Nick a bad influence, or a good one? She had some thinking to do.

Start reading at the *on page 84.*

Chrissy looked deep into Nick's eyes. His eyelashes were long and thick, like an attractive llama-human hybrid. She had never seen eyelashes on anyone that thick, unless you count the time when on a hunting trip with her dad as a child she shot a deer, and afterward, approached its heaving body just in time to watch the light slowly fade from its eyes—its thickly eyelashed eyes. Watching that deer die—her first experience with death, really—had such a profound effect on Chrissy that for the rest of her life, she would seriously consider maybe doing meatless Mondays.

Chrissy shook her head. Now was not the time to be thinking of dead deer.

"Whatcha thinking about?" Nick whispered.

The moment had come. Forget candy canes, forget Cole, forget this whole mess of a year. She closed her eyes and leaned in close, closer, closer.

"Not dead deer," she whispered back. She looked into his eyes again. Then, down to his lips. Then back to his eyes. Then back to his lips. That's how she saw people do it in the movies. She looked up at his eyes and then back down to his lips again, just for good measure. When she had repeated this a dozen or so times, she knew it was time. The moment had come. Forget candy canes, forget Cole, forget this whole mess of a year. She closed her eyes and leaned in close, closer, closer.

Any moment now, she thought, she'd feel his lips. Any moment. And then, she was choking, her mouth full of soil.

Her eyes flew open. All she saw was black. That's because she was face down, open-mouthed in the dirt. She had missed Nick's face. She pushed herself up in a panic, spitting soil everywhere and brushing dirt from her face. Nick was staring at her with his head cocked, the way he did when he saw a dog who has one of those contraptions with wheels instead of its hind legs. A look that said, I'm not quite sure what's going on or how we got to this point, but I think it's adorable?

"I'm so sorry," Chrissy sputtered. "Not trying—no kiss—just fall? Face. Face dirt. Face dirt … accident." She wasn't speaking complete sentences. Nick stared at her, the way he did when he saw a parrot who has been trained to speak in single words and phrases, but who doesn't yet understand the conventions of a complete sentence.

Chrissy's cheeks flamed red, although you couldn't see it through the dirt caked on her cheeks. Did he know she had been trying to kiss him? How embarrassing.

"Hey," Nick said, flicking a clump of mud from her nose. "Don't worry. I know exactly what happened."

"You … do?" Chrissy asked.

"Sure," Nick said, smiling. "You're a clumsy girl."

"A … clumsy girl?" Chrissy repeated.

"Yeah," said Nick warmly. "A clumsy girl. You're so breathtakingly beautiful that on your own, you'd be simply unapproachable, especially for a nice boy-next-door type like me. But then we learn about your fatal flaw, your most glaring imperfection: You're clumsy. A klutz! Accident-prone. You frequently set off a Rube Goldberg–style series of disastrous events in your apartment simply by tripping on the rug or knocking over a coffee mug. And that's not all. When there's an important client at work, someone you really need to impress, you reliably will walk confidently past him holding a large stack of binders and papers, and suddenly take a giant pratfall, your legs flying up in the air and your papers scattering everywhere. You'll struggle up to a seated position, your work ponytail disheveled, your glasses dangling halfway off your face, and whisper, 'Nobody saw that, did they?' But then you'll look up, and of course, the important client is looking right down at you—and yeah, he saw the whole thing. But here's the twist: With your glasses hanging down like that, he can see that you are not just smart with glasses, but that, improbably, you are also hot without glasses. So he'll smile in a way that says he thought it was adorable. And guess what? That's right: You're getting the account. Basically, when it comes down to it, 50 percent of your personality is that you're adorably clumsy, and the other 50 percent is that you write about fashion for your magazine, but what you really want to do is write about war, which, as the editors have stressed many times, is not something a fashion magazine about shapewear is interested in doing in any capacity."

Chrissy started to respond, but accidentally knocked over Nick's bucket of candy canes instead.

"Whoops," she said, looking straight at him. "Guess I was just clumsy."

Nick looked like he was going to say something, but Chrissy stopped him.

Start reading at the *below.*

"I think—I have—it's time for me … goodbye, Nick," she said.

Nick flopped backward into the dirt again, content, covered in snowflakes. If Chrissy had looked back as she walked away, she would have seen that two of his abs were poking out beneath his shirt. But instead, she just hurried inside and slammed the door.

"Next time, guys," Nick whispered to his stomach muscles.

SCENE
5

THE DRAMATIC
MIX-UP

Chrissy did not have a crush on Nick. That's what she would tell herself in the mirror every morning, the way you do when you definitely don't have a crush on someone.

So maybe it would be more appropriate to say that Chrissy wouldn't let herself *admit* that she had a crush on Nick. When she saw him around her mom's house, she smiled and said hi, but that was it—she would hurry off to wherever she was headed next, never letting the conversation go too far. It wasn't just that she was still giddy from and embarrassed by their last encounter in the candy cane fields. It was also that she was just out of a long-term relationship. Her heart was still a little broken over Cole, but even if it hadn't been, now just wasn't the time to get mixed up with someone new. So as much as she could, she avoided Nick.

Still, Nick kept finding ways to let her know he was thinking of her.

Should Nick ...

 Express his feelings through candy canes? *Turn to page 88 and start reading at the candy cane.*

 Show Chrissy he's thinking of her with peppermint bark? *Turn to page 88 and start reading at the sun.*

 Try to win her heart by saying the six words every woman wants to hear? *Turn to page 90 and start reading at the heart.*

Like the night she came back to her room to find a candy cane on the pillow. Or the night after that, when she found that her towels had been folded into candy cane shapes. Or the night after that, when all her bedding had been changed to red and white stripes. Or the night after *that*, when she found that he had painted diagonal red stripes across her mother's vintage wedding dress, an heirloom that Chrissy had been saving to wear at her own wedding. Chrissy pretended to be annoyed, but secretly, she was flattered.

Start reading at the *on page 91.*

Like the morning Chrissy woke up to the sound of screams from downstairs. She bolted upright in bed in a panic, just in time to hear the front door slam and footsteps pound up the stairs.

"Chrissy, it's amazing!" her mother was yelling, her voice getting closer and closer. "Chrissy, wake up, you've got to see this!" The door to Chrissy's room burst open.

"Mom!" Chrissy cried, pulling the covers up to her neck. "Whatever happened to knocking?"

Chrissy's mom waved her off, still trying to catch her breath.

"The trees, Chrissy!" she panted. "It's … a miracle! You've got to … come see!"

"Can you please give me a minute to get dressed, then?" Chrissy asked. "I'd appreciate some privacy."

"Oh, this privacy thing again," her mom said, waving her off. "This is the diary incident of 2003 all over again."

"You read my diary!" Chrissy cried, suddenly remembering. "You were snooping!"

"I was not!" her mother replied, indignantly. "It's like I told you: I was cleaning under your bed, and the diary just happened to fall open to the page where you confessed your darkest secrets!"

"We both know that you read more than one page," Chrissy said.

"Well if I did, it wasn't on purpose," her mom insisted. "What, is it my fault that just as I was finished accidentally reading the first page, a gust of wind came in through your bedroom window and just happened to blow it open to the next page?"

"Mom!" Chrissy said. "Please just wait in the hallway. I'll be out in a minute."

Chrissy emerged from her room a minute later, fully dressed but still yawning.

"Okay," she said, "what was this you were saying about miracle trees?"

"You'll see," Chrissy's mom said. "Follow me."

They walked down the stairs and out the front door, across the porch and into the yard.

"Here," Chrissy's mom said, walking up to one of the oldest trees on their property. "Look at the birch. There's something going on with the bark."

"What, that it peels off?" Chrissy asked, approaching the tree. "Everyone knows about that." Suddenly, she froze, staring at the tree. Slowly, she reached out, tentatively touching the white bark. Brow furrowed, she brought her fingers back to her lips and licked them. They tasted like …

"White chocolate," her mom said, licking her own fingers and nodding. "And peppermint."

She was right, Chrissy thought, staring at the tree. Somehow, all the bark on their white birch had been replaced with … peppermint bark.

"It's my favorite Christmas treat," Chrissy said. "But who could have …"

Suddenly, she remembered: The other day, she had heard Nick out back on the phone with someone. He had been saying, "And you're sure this brand of frosting is strong enough to adhere peppermint bark to a birch tree?" At the time, she hadn't thought a thing of it. But now …

Chrissy smiled and shook her head. She couldn't quite explain it, but for some reason, she had a sneaking suspicion that somehow–somehow–Nick was involved here.

She broke off another piece of peppermint bark and took a bite. Yum, thought Chrissy. It was the perfect combination of white chocolate and peppermint, with a little bit of super-adhesive frosting to balance everything out.

Start reading at the *on page 91.*

Like the one day that Nick and Chrissy passed each other in the kitchen and Nick stopped her.

"Hey, Chrissy," he said, looking thoughtful. "There's something I think you should know."

"Okay," Chrissy said slowly.

"*Die Hard* isn't a Christmas movie," Nick said simply. "And look, I know you and I are just getting to know each other, but I want to be up front about where I stand on the important issues. And that's just how I feel: *Die Hard* isn't a Christmas movie. And thinking that it is isn't a personality trait. See you around!" He waved and walked out the back door.

The butterflies that had been resting in Chrissy's stomach took flight.

Start reading at the *on page 91.*

BUILD YOUR OWN CHRISTMAS MOVIE ROMANCE

"He's sweet, and he's cute, but I just don't know if I'm ready," Chrissy told her best friend Holly on the phone. Holly hasn't come up before in this book because she wasn't necessary as a narrative device until now, but trust me, behind the scenes, she's been involved the whole time, just doing a lot of classic best friend things. (You should see their text chains.)

"Come on, Holly," Chrissy said. "Help me out. What do you think I should do?"

Should Holly be ...

 Chrissy's sarcastic best friend from the city? *Turn to page 92 and start reading at the skyscrapers.*

 Chrissy's friend whose answer to any problem is shopping? *Turn to page 93 and start reading at the shopping bag.*

 Talking to Chrissy while simultaneously trying to hold another conversation? *Turn to page 95 and start reading at the balloons.*

"You know what else is sweet and cute?" Holly asked. "A nectarine with googly eyes glued on it. And do you know what makes a terrible husband?" She paused dramatically for effect.

"A nectarine with googly eyes glued on it," she concluded.

"Come on," Chrissy said, "I really need your help here. What do I do about Nick?"

"Ew," said Holly. "First of all, we can't forget the fact that he's a townie."

"I know," admitted Chrissy. "He's a genuine, born-and-bred Candy Cane Falls townie."

"So if you got together," Holly continued, "that would mean … what? You'd never come back to New York? You'd waste away in Candy Cane Falls? I mean, you may as well move to the moon; or worse," she paused in disgust, "… Queens."

"I wouldn't call it 'wasting away,'" Chrissy countered, but she would be lying if she hadn't thought the same thing. She *liked* doing business in the city, where many businesses and buildings were. What would she do in Candy Cane Falls? There weren't any business buildings there. She crinkled up her nose.

"Don't crinkle up your nose like," Holly said. "I can hear you doing it through the phone. It makes you look like one of those bald Sphinx cats."

Chrissy tried to relax her face. How did Holly know?

"You know," Chrissy said, "I'm kind of going through something here, and some encouragement would be nice."

"Sorry, Chris," Holly said. "You know I love you. But you also know that I pride myself on being brutally honest. That's my whole thing! I've taken my decision to deploy casual, off-putting cruelty toward everyone in my life, and I've somehow successfully rebranded myself into someone who just 'tells it like it is.'"

> *"I've taken my decision to deploy casual, off-putting cruelty toward everyone in my life, and I've somehow successfully rebranded myself into someone who just 'tells it like it is.'"*

"That's remarkably self-aware," said Chrissy, "but just this once, couldn't you–"

"If you want someone to make you feel better," Holly interrupted, "talk to a doctor. If you want someone to tell you the truth, talk to me."

"But *you're* a doctor," Chrissy replied. "A pediatric neurosurgeon."

"I have very poor bedside manner," Holly conceded. "But you have to admit it: You love me! I say things like, 'We'll be best friends forever because you already know too much.' I have, like, six 'Fluent in Sarcasm' coffee mugs because people are always giving them to me, saying, 'This made me think of you!' I'm just a whole situation of a person!"

"So you're saying I should let the whole Nick thing go," Chrissy said.

"I'm just saying," Holly said, "that it's like my favorite Henry Ford quote: 'Whether you think you can, or you think you can't … you can't.'"

"I don't think that's how the quote goes," Chrissy said.

"Look," Holly continued. "I'm just here to act as a sounding board and drive the plot along, so I'm going to let you go. Talk to you never. Big city forever!"

"Big city forever," Chrissy mumbled.

Start reading at the *on page 97.*

"Girl," said Holly, "I know exactly what a situation like this calls for." She paused for dramatic effect. "Shopping!"

Then the line went completely silent.

"Holly?" Chrissy asked after some time had passed. "Are you still there?"

"Ah, sorry!" Holly cried. "If we had been together in real life, or in a movie, that would have been the part where we went into our shopping montage, where, like, you'd come out of the dressing room once, and I'd shake my head, like, 'No, wrong outfit,' and then you'd emerge again in new clothing, and I'd roll my eyes and shake my head even harder, like, 'No, still wrong outfit,' but then you'd come out a third time, and I would nod my head vigorously and high-five you, like, 'Now that's what I'm talkin' about!' But," she concluded, "we're on the phone."

"A shopping montage would be fun," Chrissy admitted.

"You know the only thing that helps when I'm bummed that I can't have a shopping montage?" Holly asked.

"What?" Chrissy responded.

"Shopping!" Holly cried.

Silence again.

"Holly …" Chrissy said.

"Sorry, I did it again! I'm getting distracted," Holly apologized. "Let's talk about Nick. What do you think you should do?"

"Honestly, I don't know," Chrissy admitted. "I mean, I just got out of a long-term relationship. I don't know if it's even a good idea to even be thinking about dating someone right now. And that's assuming he even wants to date me! I mean, he's flirty, but I don't actually know how he feels."

"That's really tough," Holly said. "And I'm sorry to say this," she paused.

"But," she started again.

"And stop me if I've suggested this before," she continued.

"And remember, this advice is coming from my therapist, not just from me," she added.

"But again," she restated.

"I really think," she took a deep breath.

"There's only one thing to do," she exhaled.

"Shopping," she concluded finally.

"Okay, Holly, I'm going to let you go," Chrissy said. "My phone is about to die."

"You know what I do when my battery gets low?" Holly asked.

"What?" Chrissy sighed.

"I go shopping!" Holly cried. "In part because of the emotional release, but in part to get a more effective charger. Good luck with Nick! Let me know what mall you end up going to."

"Bye, Holly," Chrissy said, and hung up. She sighed.

Start reading at the *on page 97.*

"You know what I think you should do?" Holly asked.

"Tell me," Chrissy begged.

"Remember the ground is lava!" Holly screamed.

"What?" Chrissy responded in confusion.

"Sorry, Chris," Holly apologized, "I'm at the park with the kids and things are getting intense. Let me ask you: How are you feeling about everything with Cole? I mean, that breakup is pretty fresh."

"I don't know that I'm over it," admitted Chrissy, "but also honestly haven't been thinking about him as much since I've been in Candy Cane Falls. Don't you think that ... means something?"

"I think it means that mulch is for walking in, not for eating, get the mulch out of your mouth right now, young lady! I don't know, Chrissy, do you think it means something?"

"It feels important," Chrissy admitted, "but maybe I'm just reading into things."

"How old are you?" Holly snapped.

"Uh, 32?" Chrissy responded. "Ugh, you're right. I know I'm being immature about all of this."

"Where is your mother?"

"I … think she's downstairs," Chrissy said, confused. "You're right, maybe I should ask her for advice. I hate to admit it, but she's actually pretty good at–"

"Do you think she'll be happy to find out that you like to bully younger children?"

"Well, hey," Chrissy protested, "Nick may be, like, six months younger than me, but I'd hardly call him a child. And besides, I wouldn't really say I've been bullying him, maybe just–"

"You're coming with me," Holly snapped.

"I'd love to," Chrissy sighed. "I miss you a lot."

"And we're going to track down your mother," she continued.

"Again, I think she's downstairs, but you're right, I should find out for sure, and I'm sure you would be helpful," Chrissy agreed.

"And we're going to tell her that you've been trapping small children in the tube slides and farting on them," Holly continued.

"Oh," Chrissy said. "I now see what has been happening here."

"Chrissy, I'm so sorry, but I have to let you go," Holly said, panting. "I have a fart bandit with me and I need to report him to his mother. Tell me if you end up falling in love with Nick, okay? And if you keep falling down I will carry you, don't think I won't."

"Thanks," Chrissy whispered, tearing up.

"What?" Holly said. "Oh, sorry, Chris, I didn't realize you were still on the line. This kid's gone boneless. I'm going to have to carry him until we find his mom. Talk soon!"

Chrissy hung up the phone and closed her eyes.

Start reading at the *below.*

She needed to take a walk to clear her head. She had so much to think about.

She walked downstairs, opened the front door, and gasped. Standing in front of her stood Cole, dressed in a business suit, holding a bouquet of business flowers (marigolds, bluebottles, acacias: the MBA bouquet). His arm was raised, just about to knock.

"What … what are you doing here?" Chrissy stammered.

Cole cleared his throat. He looked nervous.

"Is there somewhere we can talk?" he asked.

"Here is fine," Chrissy said. She was in shock. Part of her was overwhelmed by how good it felt to see Cole—it had been so long since she'd seen a proper cufflink, and her health was suffering for it; but the other part of her thought, how dare he show up like this, unannounced?

"On … the porch? Are you serious?" Cole asked, looking around.

Chrissy stood examining him, expressionless.

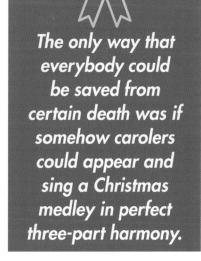

The only way that everybody could be saved from certain death was if somehow carolers could appear and sing a Christmas medley in perfect three-part harmony.

"Okay," he said nervously, pulling a crumpled piece of paper from his pocket. "The porch. By the way," he said, admiring the floorboards, "how did your mom get the condo association to approve them painting a concrete porch to look like real wood?"

"This is real wood," said Chrissy. "And there aren't any condo associations in Candy Cane Falls. Well, there used to be one, and the members really didn't get along. The only things they had in common were that they ran the condo association and that all three of them loved to sing. It was just nothing but drama between them until a few years ago when there was an emergency down at the middle school on Christmas Eve and, well—long story short— the only way that everybody could be saved from certain death was if somehow carolers could appear and sing a Christmas medley in perfect three-part harmony, and anyway, this was all going down on the same night that the condo board was about to close a huge business deal, but in the end, they decided that Christmas spirit mattered more than making money and buying groceries, so they rushed down to the middle school, sang the medley, and everyone was saved. Anyway," Chrissy finally took a deep breath, "they basically disassembled the condo association after that to focus on Christmas caroling full-time."

Cole looked like he was going to faint. "You're telling me that they're currently caroling … full-time … for their jobs?"

"Yes."

"And you're sure that CAROL doesn't actually stand for, like, cost analysis report optimization logistician?"

"I'm sure," said Chrissy. "Well, 98 percent sure. Actually, I heard that this year they're training for a caroling contest with a big cash prize. It's the exact amount needed, incidentally, to pay what it would cost to rebuild the beloved advent calendar shop owned by Old Mr. Bailey, a staple of the community, a kind, older man who had become such a father figure to so many in the town that he was more affectionately known as 'Feliz Navidad,' but like, with an emphasis on 'Dad,' and who, after the tragic loss of his wife—who died heroically saving the town's children from a roaring tinsel fire—has had nothing to live for but the shop. The twist? The judge of the contest is none other than Marv Meisterburger, the alto caroler's vindictive ex-boyfriend. What will she do? I guess we'll see. But I have a feeling that Old Mr. Bailey may have a few tricks up his plush red sleeve yet," Chrissy finished with a wink.

"What are you doing?" Cole asked, staring at her in horror.

"I don't know," Chrissy said, shaking her head. "Sorry, I kind of blacked out there for a second. It happens when I spend too much time away from a robust public transit system. Anyway. What were you saying?"

Cole started to unfold the letter that he still held crumpled in his hand.

"I have a few things I need to say," he started.

"Wait," said Chrissy holding out her hand.

Should Chrissy ...

 Let Cole read the letter? *Turn to page 100 and start reading at the pencil.*

 Tell Cole that she needs some time alone to think? *Turn to page 102 and start reading at the gingerbread man.*

"Never mind," said Chrissy, shaking her head. "Sorry, go ahead. Read the letter."

Cole cleared his throat and began to read.

Dear Chrissy,

I have been trying to find the words to explain how I truly feel about you. I would say 'I love you,' but that feels too simple and straightforward. And I always told myself that if I met the woman I loved, I wouldn't just tell her I loved her: I would woo her with a series of office product–related similes. So, Chrissy:

Without you, my heart is like the copier on the fourth floor: broken.

Without you, my soul is like sensitive documents fed through the PowerChop 9000: shredded.

Without you, I am like a stapler without staples: empty.

Without you, I am like one of those pieces of generic hotel art, still in its shrink-wrap, that you use to decorate your office walls: depressing.

Without you, I am like a pencil after you just slammed the pencil down on your desk in anger because you made some money, but not a *lot* of money: pointless.

Without you, I am like a blue whiteboard marker: blue.

Without you, my accomplishments feel like my Slack chat when I just need a break from the chatter: minimized.

Without you, I am like that whoopie cushion you got one year for Secret Santa, which you immediately stabbed with a pair of scissors because you hate Christmas and mischief, and Julie, who got your name, didn't realize: deflated.

Without you, my memory of our time together is like using a Sharpie to write on a whiteboard: It cannot be erased.

Without you, I am like a piece of generic Scotch tape and two pieces of literally anything: barely holding it together.

Without you, I remember how, not unlike a fine powder used in laser printers, compared to my other ex-girlfriends, your arms were just: toner.

Without you, I am like two pieces of construction paper held together by a dried-out glue stick: it's clear; we aren't together

I guess what I'm saying is that I love you, and I want you back, and I also as I write this, I am sitting at your old desk, just kind of looking around at the physical objects remaining in your office. You left a lot behind. If it's okay with you, I'm stealing the rubber band ball.

Warm regards,

Cole

Senior Management at Big Business Company

*** *"Whether you think you can, or you think you can't, you're right."* - Henry Ford ***

*** *"Mo' money, FEWER problems."* - Me ***

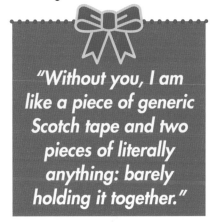

"Without you, I am like a piece of generic Scotch tape and two pieces of literally anything: barely holding it together."

When he was done reading, Cole folded the paper back up and put it in his pocket. He looked at Chrissy expectantly.

"Well?" he said.

Chrissy's head was reeling.

"That's … a lot of similes to sort through," she finally managed. "Is it okay if I have some time to think?"

Cole's face fell, but he nodded anyway.

"Okay," he said, with a false brightness. "Sure."

Start reading at the *on page 103.*

"I'm sorry, Cole," Chrissy said, holding out her hand. "I appreciate whatever you're trying to do here. And I'm sure that whatever is in that letter contains a lot of rudimentary connections between love and office supplies, which will kind of miss the mark emotionally, but which I will find sweet nonetheless. You know, kind of like when a six-year-old gives you, like, the ring from his Ring Pop for your birthday. Like, it's fundamentally a bad gift, but there's still something sweet about it."

"How did you know about the office supply similes?" Cole asked, staring down at the paper in his hands.

"It's kind of your thing," Chrissy admitted. "Do you remember the first Valentine's Day card you made me?"

"Sure," said Cole. "It said, 'On this Valentine's Day, just like the buttons I push in the break room vending machine to get Frito's Honey BBQ Flavor Twists, the world's most underrated snack: B9.'"

"Because all this time, you thought that when people said, 'Be Mine' on Valentine's Day, they were actually saying, 'B9,'" Chrissy said. "So there was a lot going on there."

"Oh!" said Cole, "And then the first time I asked if you wanted to explore polyamory, I made you that card that said, 'Chrissy, Let's make our relationship like the 27 incognito tabs on your computer: open.'"

"Yes," Chrissy said, pursing her lips. "That was a day I felt good about our relationship."

"And then the follow-up to the card I made, when I did the joke with 'scissors'—"

"I remember, Cole," Chrissy said, cutting him off. "My point is, you have a pattern. And maybe I'll be ready to hear what you have to say in that letter soon, but you're just going to have to give me some time."

Start reading at the *on page 103.*

"So this is your mom's house, then?" Cole asked, after a pause. "Where does she do business and have meetings?" Two years of dating, and somehow he had managed to avoid coming to Candy Cane Falls until now.

"She doesn't really do that," Chrissy explained.

Cole poked his head inside the front door. "I mean, surely there's a conference room in here or … or something."

Chrissy shook her head. If Cole had just wanted to give her a letter, he could have mailed it, or emailed it, which was what they called it in Candy Cane Falls when an elf courier delivered letters to your doorstep. Why show up in person?

"Cole. What are you actually doing here?" she asked again.

Cole straightened his back.

"I'm here to ask you two things," he said. "The first question is from Big Business Company. I'm here to let you know that if you're still up for it, there's a junior executive position with your name on it. Specifically, 'Junior Executive Chrissy.' They always knew they never should have let you go; they especially knew it when profits immediately dipped. So they'd love you to come back."

Chrissy clapped her hand over her mouth.

"And the second question," Cole continued, "is a question I should have asked a long time ago."

He dropped to one knee.

"Chrissy Kristen Christopher, will you marry me?"

Should Chrissy ...

 Say "yes"? *Start reading at the stocking below.*

 **Stop for a second to think about it?** *Turn to page 107 and start reading at the bow.*

Chrissy gasped. All of her frustrations at Cole vanished instantly, as instantly as a middle-class person vanishes from Whole Foods when she realizes that the sample trays are empty. Chrissy smirked. That was one of the things she loved about Cole: She was always inspired to silently make fun of middle-class people in his presence.

"Chrissy?" Cole asked, looking up at her from the porch. "Any thoughts?"

"Sorry," Chrissy said, smiling, "I was making jokes about middle-class people in my head and got distracted."

Cole grinned. "Was it one of those ones where the joke is about how the only reason middle-class people go into Whole Foods is to get free samples, and even if they make a big show of browsing the aisle before beelining it to the sample station, we all know that it's just an act and they're only there for the samples?" he asked.

"It's performative shopping!" she responded, indignantly. "There's no need to pretend you're here to buy Guac-Kale-Mole!"

"Right, it's like, you mean to tell me you're going to spend $8 on a mango, Mrs. Minivan?" Cole asked, starting to giggle. "Come on, Mrs. Minivan. The sample station is all out of broken pieces of bruschetta. Go back to Trader Joe's, where you belong."

By this point, they were both in tears laughing. This is what she had missed, all those nights that she and Cole had spent apart on business travel. No one knew her like Cole did, not really. This, she thought, this is the kind of thing you build a life on. She was still in joke mode, and almost transitioned to a new bit about middle-class throw pillows where she was trying to decide whether the punchline would land better if she referenced Home Goods or Wayfair, when she remembered that Cole was still kneeling on the porch, waiting for an answer.

She took another breath, exhaled quickly, and then nodded.

"Yes," she said, "my answer is yes."

"Oh wow, that's—wait, but to which part?" Cole said. "I now realize I asked you a couple of yes/no questions."

"All of it," Chrissy said, nodding, "the job, the proposal, all of it. Yes. I say yes."

Beaming, Cole slipped a ring on her finger and rose to his feet. They started to kiss, until Cole pulled back and said, "You're sure about this? You know, I was kind of afraid you'd come to Candy Cane Falls and have, like, a series of epiphanies that left you fundamentally changed as a person. So, like … you mean it? You really, actually mean it when you say 'yes'?"

"I mean that 'yes' more now than I do when someone asks me if I want to turn my money into more money," said Chrissy.

"That's the most romantic thing I've ever heard," Cole said. "Want to get out of here?"

Chrissy nodded. "Now," she said, making a beeline for Cole's car. "Let's get out of here now."

"You don't want to pack a bag or something?" Cole asked, jogging after her.

"I'll buy a new wardrobe," Chrissy said, pulling the door open and sliding into the passenger seat. "All my clothes smell like peppermint now anyway."

The two sped off into the distance, and it was only on the flight home that Chrissy realized she had forgotten to say goodbye to her mom and to Nick.

Cole and Chrissy were married later that year. It was a classy wedding with few personal touches, save the slight edit in their vows, when they pledged to love each other "for richer or richer." They eventually moved into a big penthouse, one of those big, open, minimalist situations where the walls and the furniture and basically everything is white, except for, like, maybe one weird red sculpture in a corner; it was the type of home that would be featured on Apartment Therapy, and regular people would click through pictures and would feel jealous of how clean and crisp everything looked, but then later would stop and think, "But wait, where is literally any of their stuff?"

Chrissy and Cole stayed in their penthouse in the city forever, and they became richer and fancier every year. Were they happy? No one can ever know that about another couple, not really. The best I can say is that they became the type of couple who had a pair of purebred Italian Greyhounds that they dressed in argyle sweaters, and whom they referred to both in public and private as "the children," which their friends found strange, most especially because at that point, Chrissy and Cole had actual human children of their own.

Chrissy became the president of Big Business Company. Cole got super into rich-people hobbies, like doomsday prepping and playing big-city polo, which is basically like regular polo, but since there's limited space in the city, the players ride on miniature horses.

And every year on Christmas, they left the country and went skiing.

The End

BUILD YOUR OWN CHRISTMAS MOVIE ROMANCE

Chrissy took a deep breath. Her mind was racing, ping-ponging between Cole and Nick, Nick and Cole. Slow down, she told herself. Take a second to think about it. There's no hurry. What's the worst thing that ever came from someone waiting a long while before answering a question?

Before Chrissy could answer Cole, she heard a noise from the side of the house. She turned to see Nick staring at them, holding a bouquet of candy canes with a ribbon tied around them. He stared at her and Cole for a few more seconds, then the bouquet fell from his hands, and he turned and ran, leaving candy canes shattered on the ground behind him.

"No, wait, Nick!" Chrissy called, running to the side of the house. "Come back!"

But Nick was gone.

Cole was still on one knee on the front porch.

"Cole, I … I have a lot to think about," Chrissy called back toward the porch. "Is it okay if I have some more time by myself before answering?"

Cole stood up and brushed off his suit. He looked annoyed.

"If you need me," he said, "I'll be in the Naughty-or-Nice Suite at the Second Best Western."

He spun on his heel and marched back to his car, a red sports car with a custom license plate reading "WRNG4U." He slammed on the gas and the wheels spun, kicking up dirt and snow, splattering the Christmas decorations with mud. Then, just as suddenly as he had arrived, he was gone.

And so was Nick.

SCENE
6

THE PINING
MONTAGE

Chrissy sat in the living room, staring out the window. A very sad, minor-key version of "We Wish You a Merry Christmas" played in the background. It was from an old record of her dad's, one called Bummer Versions of Your Favorite Christmas Tunes for Setting the Scene Emotionally.

"More like we *don't* wish you a merry Christmas," Chrissy muttered. She held up one of her hands and then slapped it with the other. "Good one, Chrissy," she said to her herself, like a person who is doing well.

She put her head into her hands and stared out the window. Then she crossed her arms and stared out the window. Then she leaned her head against it. She was trying to find the pose that would look as sad as she felt. Finally, she settled on leaning her head against the window with her arms crossed, while moving her head in such a way that it wrote the word "sad" in the fog on the glass.

What was she going to do? She had blown it with Nick, that much was clear. She did not need to have a follow-up conversation with him to know that for sure. They had had a misunderstanding, and that was simply that. There was no chance of giving him a call and letting him know what the actual situation was and seeing if they could talk through it; the very idea made her laugh! No, Nick was gone for good. Goodbye forever, Nick.

But did she want to be with Cole? Just a few weeks ago, she would have said yes, absolutely. But that was before Nick, before Candy Cane Falls, before all of this. Had she … changed?

She needed to do some serious thinking.

Should Chrissy …

Walk back to the porch to do her thinking? *Turn to page 110 and start reading at the candle.*

Go to her Serious Thinking Spot to do her thinking? *Turn to page 113 and start reading at the mitten.*

She needed some fresh air to clear her head. So she turned off the record player then tore down all of the depressing Christmas decor she had hastily put up to set the mood for her pouting: a blown-glass Santa figurine seated by the phone, looking worried (the piece was called "Santa Waits to Hear about His Test Results"); the half-sized replica of Santa's sleigh, exactly how it's depicted in books and movies, except that attached to the reins was a court-ordered breathalyzer steering wheel lock; and of course, the famous inspirational poster that features a photo of a cat hanging from a branch and text that reads, "Hang in there," except that in this version, everything is basically the same except that the cat … is no longer in the photo. And if you're tempted to think, "Maybe it's implying that the cat was rescued, or that he escaped," that's just because you haven't noticed that pictured in the top left corner of the poster is a tiny ambulance, quickly approaching. That one wasn't Christmas-y, but it was on theme.

When she was done with all of that, she bundled back up and walked outside, only to see that Cole's car was once again parked on the street.

She marched up to the car and knocked loudly on the window. Cole rolled it down.

"What are you doing here?" she asked. "I thought you left."

"I did," Cole admitted. "But then I realized that check-in at the hotel isn't for another few hours, and also if you changed your mind, I'd have no way of knowing because my phone doesn't get service here. So I drove back and thought I'd just camp out and wait."

Chrissy was about to respond when she saw something else: a young, attractive woman was seated in the passenger seat next to Cole.

Chrissy's jaw dropped.

"And who," she asked, poking her head through the driver's side window, "is that?"

Cole looked embarrassed.

"I hired her," he admitted. "From one of those websites where you can hire someone to pose as your girlfriend for a wedding or event typically taking place during the holiday season. It's a purely PG situation. You might think it sounds silly, but these websites are real and they exist and people use them all the time."

"So why is she here?" Chrissy asked, still staring at the woman.

"Well, the idea was that if you said no to my proposal, I would come back and have her pretend to be my girlfriend to make you jealous. But it's funny," he said, turning to smile at the woman.

"Wait, what's her name?" Chrissy interrupted, pointing at the woman. "You, what's your name?"

"Honestly, it doesn't matter," Cole reassured Chrissy, cutting the woman off as she started to respond. "She was either going to serve as your two-dimensional foil, or she would be utilized briefly to redirect the plot, which kind of appears to be what's happening here. So there's just no need to get weighed down with things like her name. If you spent more time with her, you'd know more about her personality, like blonde, and sunglasses, and snapping bubble gum, and tight leather pants, and acrylic nails, and cruel. But for now," he concluded, "you can just call her whatever you want. Maybe something like Jezebel?"

"Jezebel," Chrissy repeated.

"Ivy," the woman called. "My name is Ivy."

"Anyway," Cole continued, ignoring her, "like I was saying. It was so funny—I only hired Jezebel to make you jealous. It was supposed to be for a long weekend, nothing more. And why would it be? I was hung up on you; Jezebel could tell you that. Boy, has she listened to me blather on and on all about you, and about business, and about my feelings, and I won't even get into my business feelings! And even though her online profile said, 'We won't be getting emotionally close,' it sort of seemed like we might be? Anyway, a lot happened— several goofy travel montages; an incident where I got ice cream on my nose and she kind of adorably swooped it off and we had this moment of lingering eye contact until finally I coughed and said, 'Hey, I really should get going,' and she immediately said, 'Yeah, me too, me too"; and then finally, a really rough night where I was so broken up about you, and she counseled me with incredible advice that was not only wise, but that—while on the surface seemed to be encouraging me to go for it with you—could also, if you were listening closely, be construed as her telling *me* I should go for it with *her*."

Jezebel took a sip from a tall corporate coffee cup.

"If she was your foil," Cole explained, "then this whole time, she'd be drinking something annoying like a 'double half-caf, extra whip, double the smell, three shots of grande, half-soy, but leave out soy, I'm allergic,' just to really show that, like, yikes, she's the worst. But right now she's adorable, so she's actually drinking something adorable, like maybe tea?"

"So are you two together?" Chrissy asked. "Didn't you literally just propose to me? Wait a minute," she said, a look of horror crossing her face. "Was she in the car when you proposed to me?"

"Oh, no, no," Cole reassured her, laughing. "She knew that I was doing the whole proposal thing and decided she would do some shopping in town while she waited. When I first dropped her off, I saw that she had 'Everywhere' by Michelle Branch cued up to play on her phone, so I think that maybe she just wanted some alone time to do some deep thinking about us. But no, to answer your question, we aren't together. I haven't come to my senses yet. I'm still totally hung up on you. Honestly, it's going to have to take a real eleventh-hour realization for me to understand that actually the person I was meant to be with this whole time was Jezebel."

Chrissy realized she had more thinking to do than ever. Cole and Jezebel's strange presence outside the house meant the porch was now off-limits, so only one place remained.

Start reading at the *on page 113.*

She'd go to the same place she did whenever she had serious thinking to do: her Serious Thinking Spot.

Not ten minutes later, and Chrissy was lacing up her ice skates, staring out at the frozen lake. She sighed, happily. There was nothing better than a good skate to clear her mind.

Chrissy eased out onto the lake. It had been years since she'd been skating. She'd been too busy assembling action items and thinking about the bottom line to even bother in New York. There was the big rink outside of Rockefeller Center, but one look at all of the bulky, non-black sweaters

> *What wasn't perfect, she thought, was the situation she was in. Did she want Nick? Or did she want Cole?*

and one listen to all of the "Ope, sorry!"s and "I forgive you for bumping into me, that's the neighborly way!"s and she knew: Everyone on that rink was a midwestern tourist. Plus, once she'd been walking past a busy cafe in Manhattan when she heard a group of professionals laughing. One of the women said, "Ice skating?! What a small town, non-business thing to do!" Ever since, she'd been embarrassed of what used to be her favorite hobby.

But now, as she sliced across the ice, cutting loops and twirls, all of it came back to her. It was just like riding a bike. A very cold, slippery bike without wheels. She leapt in the air and spun; for a moment, she was breathless, and then, relief. A perfect landing!

What wasn't perfect, she thought, was the situation she was in. Nice transition, she said to herself. Maybe when she figured all of this out, she would be a writer. But for now, the question: Did she want Nick? Or did she want Cole?

Cole represented everything she loved about her life in New York City: He was tall, like a building. His hair-sprayed hair was hard, like a sidewalk. He ran really inconsistently, like the subway. But more than that, she loved how sophisticated she felt when she was with him. She loved having coffee dates where they both just clacked away on their laptops, never once making eye contact, but occasionally slapping each other a high-five. She liked walking briskly with him, comparing briefcase reviews, and going to the nicest, mostly dimly lit restaurants where the servings were so small that they could not be seen with the naked eye. She liked the way he looked in suits, and the way he defended himself in lawsuits. For a busy business lady in New York, she couldn't imagine a better partner.

And then there was Nick. Nick represented a slower, calmer life, one where she could imagine herself watching the sun go down from a porch swing, admiring the way the light danced off the candy cane fields. He maybe didn't have much need for business suits, but the way that he wore rolled-up flannels and chunky fishermen's sweaters certainly suited him just fine. (She gave herself a little high-five for the suit pun.) Plus, he was kind and generous and funny, and his abs were so nice they almost made her mad.

It was a dilemma.

 Get some advice from a mysterious stranger? *Start reading at the Santa hat below.*

 Keep thinking and skating? *Turn to page 117 and start reading at the skate.*

Suddenly, she heard a cheery voice behind her.

"Did someone say 'dilemma'?"

Chrissy spun around to face the voice. She was so frightened, though, that she kept on spinning: once, twice, three times. Without meaning to, she had accidentally just completed a move that was known in the ice-skating-while-thinking world as the "triple putz." Before that moment, the best accidental move Chrissy had ever pulled off at her Thinking Spot was something montage writers and amateur ice skaters call a "double toe whoops." She was pulled suddenly out of her thoughts by a strange sound. Someone was clapping.

Now, at last, she saw him: a man warming himself in front of a small fire near the edge of the lake. He was smiling and clapping.

"6.0 for artistry!" he called. "6.0 for technical merit! Bravo!"

"Actually, that scoring system hasn't been used in ice skating since 2004," Chrissy called back to the stranger. "The new system was designed to create more standardized scores and reduce the possibility of corruption, and it's much more complex. When's the last time you watched competitive ice skating, anyway? Let me guess—the 1998 winter Olympics."

"Tara Lipinski was an absolute force," the man admitted. "And Elvis Stojko did a backflip! But that's not what I'm here to discuss. I find it interesting that you're talking with me about the Olympics. I didn't come here to talk about games. I came here to talk about …"

He paused, waiting for her to complete the sentence.

"I didn't come here to talk about games," he tried again. "I came to talk about …"

He raised his eyebrows. Surely, she would get this.

"Abs?" he finally prompted.

"Nick!" Chrissy gasped. But before she had a chance to think about how odd it was that this strange man knew about Nick, she realized something else.

"You look familiar," she said. "Don't I know you from somewhere?"

She studied him: big, white beard; bright, twinkling eyes; red suit with white piping; black boots and belt; big burlap sack. Her eyes widened suddenly with realization.

"Kris!" she cried. "The guy who hangs out outside the stores in downtown Candy Cane Falls! You look so different."

Kris smoothed his velvety suit proudly.

"I upgraded the sweatshirt for the suit," he said, "but otherwise, you've got it. Same old me."

Chrissy couldn't stop staring at him. It was Kris, certainly—regular, old, non-magical human Kris—but there was something different about him. Something she couldn't quite put her finger on.

"I don't have much time," Kris said, squinting out at something on the ice. "As you can imagine, this time of the year is quite busy for me."

He looked at her pointedly.

"It's a busy time of year for me, specifically," he said again. "I'm sure you understand why."

Chrissy did not get where Kris was going with this. Maybe he worked at a ski resort?

Kris glanced out at the ice behind Chrissy and seemed to notice something.

"We're running out of time," he said quickly. "But I came here to say this."

He lowered his voice mysteriously.

"Sometimes," he said slowly, "things are just mint to be."

"Mint to be, Chrissy," he repeated when there was no response. "Sometimes things are mint to be. Think about it. Uh, whoa, look over there!" he suddenly shouted, pointing behind Chrissy.

She spun around to look, but saw nothing. When she turned back around, both Kris and the fire were gone.

Mint to be, he had said. Mint to be. She was going to have to think about this.

Start reading at the *on page 117.*

There was a lot to sort through. Luckily, she prided herself on her ability to prioritize. So she had just started thinking about Nick's abs again when it happened—a loud pop and snap beneath her skates. Before she could even react, the ice under her feet gave way, and she plunged into the freezing water below.

SCENE
7

THE
KISS

"Help!" Chrissy screamed. "Help, help, help!"

Chrissy thrashed about in the freezing water, craning her neck, looking desperately around the park for anyone, but her fears were quickly confirmed: There was no one else around.

She tried to hoist herself up onto the ice, but every time she did, it collapsed in pieces beneath her weight and tumbled into the cold water.

Okay, so that wasn't going to work. What should she do now? She could only tread water for so long. She started thinking about survival books she had read.

Suddenly she remembered—she was supposed to let her body go limp! She stopped treading water, relaxed her body, and immediately sank toward the bottom of the lake. She struggled to swim back to the surface, and then, finally breaking the surface, she coughed and gasped for air. Right, she remembered. The going limp thing was for quicksand, not frozen lakes. It wasn't the first time she'd been hoodwinked by advice about quicksand, and it certainly wouldn't be the last. But we simply don't have time to go into all of that right now.

What was she going to do? Her limbs were already numb with cold, and she could feel her muscles burning from keeping her above water. She was not going to last.

That's when she heard it.

A faint tinkling, like bells—that same sound she'd heard so many times since coming to Candy Cane Falls—coming from deep in the depths of the black water.

Should Chrissy ...

 Dive into the water to investigate the sound? *Turn to page 120 and start reading at the bell.*

 Keep treading water, and not, you know, submerge herself in 39-degree water? *Turn to page 121 and start reading at the thermometer.*

How many times had Chrissy heard that mysterious sound? It had been everywhere this past week: in her Uber, at her mom's house, whenever the topic of her father's tragic death was broached. In the streets, in stores, potentially at that bell concert? With that last one, it was hard to say for sure.

But it *had* to mean something, Chrissy decided. And she was going to find out. She took a deep breath, and she dove under the water.

At first, it was nothing but black murky water, but then, below her, she saw something, far in the distance: a faint light.

She swam down deeper, toward the distant light and sound of the bells, which grew louder the deeper she swam. Her lungs were burning, but still she swam, farther and farther down until the light began to take shape. It began to look less like a light, and more like … a face? A beautiful woman's face?

And finally, she saw it: It wasn't just any woman's face.

It was Candace Cameron Bure's face.

It had to be a mirage, but it also looked so lifelike that Chrissy almost wanted to reach out and touch it. She hardly had time to take in the blurry, watery details of Candace Cameron Bure's face: its warmth and openness, but also, its mutability, able to transform from beleaguered hockey mom just trying to win the cookie contest to condo development villain with the snap of a director's fingers.

You could say that she's been typecast, Chrissy started to think, but in a way, you could *also* make the argument that she has defied typecasting altogether, but she stopped that train of thought when she saw that the Candace Cameron Bure mirage was trying to say something.

Chrissy squinted in the dark, trying to read Candace Cameron Bure's lips. At last, she could just barely begin to make something out.

"Swim … to … the … surface … right … now … you … will … drown … the … bells … thing … is … not … magic … there … are … just … a … lot … of … bells … in … this … town."

What could she possibly mean? Chrissy didn't have time to figure it out. Her lungs were on fire. She swam as fast and as hard as she could back toward the surface and burst through the water.

Start reading at the (🎄) on page 123.

Chrissy shook her head. Of course there wasn't something magical that had to do with bells happening under the water. This must be one of the phases of hypothermia. First, shivering, then slow, shallow breathing, then the misguided belief that a mystical set of symbolic Christmas bells have been following you to teach you an important lesson, and then drowning.

No. She was just going to keep treading water.

Minutes went by. Five, ten, twenty. Her arms and legs were leaden, heavy, numb. She'd lost the ability to feel her hands and feet. It was getting harder and harder to keep her neck above water. She didn't want to give up, but something inside of her was beginning to. She was so cold, and so, so tired.

To stay alert, she tried to think of her favorite inspirational business quotes.

"There can't be user-centric metrics without we-ser-centric metrics."

"Never forget someone who reminded you of what your core competency was."

"A buy-in a day keeps the bankruptcy away."

It was when she couldn't remember any more quotes that she knew: This was the end. At long last, thinking of her favorite romantic comedy, *Glengarry Glen Ross*, she smiled and, with numb lips, mumbled, "Always … be … cold." She closed her eyes and slid beneath the water.

There were a few bubbles, and then the lake was still. Then suddenly, with a gasp, Chrissy came bursting back up through the surface. In the brief seconds she had spent under the water, she had had a vision.

In the brief seconds she had spent under the water, she had had a vision.

It was of a little caroler in a newsboy cap, jangling a tin cup, standing on the porch of their cabin before he vanished into the air, leaving nothing behind but the sound of tinkling bells on the worst night of Chrissy's life: the night her father had died. She had spent so much time over the last decade obsessing over the details of her father's death that Christmas in the cabin—the way the dastardly grinch snake (*Serpentes malevolus*) had found its way into the cabin; the way it had curled itself up to hide with the strings of popcorn and cranberries; the way her father reached down for a string, remarking, "This string of popcorn and cranberries sure has a *lot* of scales for having zero popcorn or cranberries"; then, the way he was struck suddenly, how Chrissy had sprinted into action, immediately grabbing the nearest phone and setting a timer for 15 minutes, because that was how long it would take her to make her family's famous snake-bite salve, a concoction derived of 0 percent medicine and 100 percent candy cane; and how the salve did not work, how Chrissy had blamed herself all these years; and how she had hated Christmas ever since as a result. And also snakes, but this one just doesn't come up too much, mostly because cute groups of little children do not typically knock on your door in December and ask if they can sing you a medley of snake songs.

But! She had been so busy thinking of all that, that she had completely forgotten the mysterious phrase the little boy had whispered before—and again, this cannot be emphasized enough—he literally magically disintegrated into the atmosphere. But when she had gone underwater, suddenly, she remembered what the boy had said. It had felt so mysterious, so coded then. What could it mean now?

"Don't drown, your boyfriends are coming," she said slowly to herself, remembering when the little boy had said those same words. "Don't drown … your boyfriends are coming."

What could it possibly mean? Perhaps it was some sort of cipher, or maybe an acrostic poem situation?

Don't drown, your boyfriends are coming. Don't drown, your boyfriends are coming.

Newly energized, she kept repeating the mysterious, unparsable phrase to herself while she treaded water. She was determined. She would stay alive at least long enough to figure out what it meant.

Don't drown; your boyfriends are coming.

Start reading at the 🎄 *below.*

And that's when she heard the voices. Two men's voices, calling for her.

"Chrissy! Chrissy?"

"Don't drown!" one of them shouted. "We're coming!"

That sounds familiar, Chrissy thought.

The shouting was coming from the woods.

"Out here!" she screamed as loud as she could.

There was a flurry of footsteps, and then, moments later, Cole and Nick burst from the trees near the edge of the lake. When they caught sight of Chrissy in the water, they both sprinted to the shore.

"Are you okay?" asked Nick. "Stay calm, I'm coming to you."

He eased his foot out on the ice, and cracks spiderwebbed out from his weight.

"It's not safe!" Chrissy said. "The ice won't hold. You'll have to try something else."

Should Cole ...

 Try to rescue Chrissy with what he thinks is an inner tube? *Start reading at the inner tube below.*

 Turn to his phone for help? *Turn to page 125 and start reading at the phone.*

"I've got it!" cried Cole, yanking his briefcase open and dropping to his knees. "I'm a hero!"

"What ... do you have?" Nick asked, looking back at Cole suspiciously.

"An inner tube!" Cole cried, tugging something out of his briefcase. "I saw it in the kitchen at Chrissy's house and thought, 'Huh, this might come in handy.' Now if you'll excuse me," he said, smirking at Nick, "I have some inner tube heroism to perform."

"Wait, that's not ..." Nick started to say, but Cole shouted over him.

"Here ... it ... comes!" Cole cried, rearing back and throwing something out across the lake toward Chrissy. "It's cylindrical! It has a hole in the middle! I found it in the kitchen around Christmas! It's ... definitely a rescue inner tube!"

BUILD YOUR OWN CHRISTMAS MOVIE ROMANCE

"It's ... definitely a fruitcake!" Chrissy called back moments later, when what had turned out to definitely be a fruitcake had smacked against the surface of the lake next to her and then immediately sunk. "It's a fruitcake," she repeated, sighing.

"Are you sure?" Cole yelled. "I really think it was an inner tube. Hold on, I'll just Google 'differences between fruit cake and inner tube.'"

"Please do something more useful!" Chrissy yelled back.

Start reading at the 📞 *below.*

"Chrissy! Stay calm! I'll figure this out," said Cole, pulling his phone out of his pocket.

Nick stepped back from the ice and dropped to the ground in a crouch, putting his head between his knees.

"Come on," he whispered to himself. "Think, think, think."

Cole stepped back toward the woods.

"Better reception!" he called. Then, looking at his phone and typing, he muttered, "Friend ... fallen ... in ice ... what ... to do ... no, that's not good, maybe how ... escape ... from ... frozen ... lake ... wiki ... no, that's not good either."

Suddenly, Nick shot to his feet.

"The candy canes!" he yelled, and ripped his backpack off. He turned it over and dumped it out; it was stocked full of freshly harvested candy canes. Freshly harvested and uncut, a hook on each end.

Quickly, he got to work, creating a giant chain of candy canes.

"You want to help here?" Nick called back to Cole, as he got busy hooking one candy cane onto another.

Cole waved him off without looking up from his phone. He was still mumbling. "Ask ... Jeeves ... how to ... save ... friend ... from ... frozen lake or pond?" He looked up. "Is this a lake or a pond?"

Nick ignored him. By that time, he'd created a chain of candy canes so long it just might reach Chrissy. He grabbed one end, gave it an expert lasso, and tossed the candy cane chain out toward Chrissy. It landed on the ice right next to her.

"Chrissy! Grab on to the candy cane rope!" Nick cried. Chrissy reached out of the water and gripped one of the striped candies in her hand.

"Got it!" she yelled.

Then she felt a tug on the line, and her body was pulled up, up, and out of the water. Nick stood on the shoreline, straining with the effort of hauling her in. The candy canes stretched and they strained, but they did not break. God, Nick thought, if only one of the mass candy cane manufacturers were here right now. I'd point to this, and I'd say, *here*. Here is the difference a homegrown candy cane makes.

Nick pulled and pulled on the candy cane rope, and, tug after tug after tug, Chrissy was slowly pulled across the ice and water. And then finally, with one final, terrific pull, Nick yanked her out of the lake and onto dry land.

He ripped off his jacket and draped it over shoulders. She was soaking wet and freezing, and couldn't stop her teeth from chattering. Nick took one look at her and then ripped his sweater off too, handing it to her. She tugged it over her head and on. Nick was now wearing just his undershirt, a white t-shirt that had a photo of two golden retrievers on it. "Who rescued *whom*?" the text below the photo read.

He took a step closer to her.

"Nice trick with the candy canes," Chrissy smiled, her teeth chattering.

"They call me the cowboy of Candy Cane Falls," he smiled back. "Or at least maybe now they will."

She inched closer to him and looked into his eyes.

"I'm not going back to New York," she said.

"You're not going back to New York," Nick repeated, and then he kissed her. He smelled like peppermint.

After a few magical, minty moments, Chrissy pulled back from the kiss to study Nick's face, but while she did, she heard a commotion behind her.

Cole had finally looked up from his phone. He sprinted over, nearly tripping over himself.

"Chrissy!" he cried. "You're okay! Sorry, I was looking for ways to rescue you, but then I went down this internet hole, and you *have* to see this video, it's from the Top 10 Most Hilarious Ice Rescue Fails, and it—"

Chrissy put her hand over Cole's mouth to shut him up, and then she kissed Nick again.

FINAL MERRY CHRISTMAS

Chrissy's childhood home was packed with people.

"Great party, Mom!" Chrissy yelled.

"What?" her mom yelled back. "It's too loud in here. I can't hear you."

"I said *great party, Mom*," Chrissy yelled even louder.

"Thanks!" her mom called back. "I got them on sale!"

What was initially supposed to be Chrissy's family Christmas dinner had instead transformed into a full-on Christmas bash. Or had it technically become a gala? No, that wasn't it, Chrissy thought to herself. What was the word she was looking for? It was on the tip of her tongue. Then she remembered: "Soirée!" she cried in excitement.

"Oh, no problem!" the man next to her responded. Chrissy looked at him in confusion, and then shrugged and moved on. That was another thing about Chrissy: She didn't know how to pronounce "soirée."

Call it whatever kind of party you want, but the fact was that it felt like half of the town had shown up that night. The friendly people of Candy Cane Falls just couldn't help it: When they heard the good news of Chrissy's miraculous ice rescue and the budding romance between her and Nick, they had to come see for themselves. This was just the kind of narrative that people in Candy Cane Falls cared deeply about, and celebrated, and forced themselves into so that they could feel like they were … part of it, I guess? Either way, Chrissy was choosing to believe that it was sweet and not actually super creepy and inappropriate, which, if she thought about it for even a moment longer, she would determine it might actually be.

But there was no time to think about that. She had a Christmas party to enjoy!

How Should This Christmas Story End?

 We discover that someone has secretly been royalty all along. *Turn to page 131 and start reading at the crown.*

 There's a mysterious knock at the door that changes the course of the whole evening. *Turn to page 135 and start reading at the stars.*

 Chrissy has a very sudden, brief epiphany. *Turn to page 139 and start reading at the ornament.*

 Chrissy discovers the secret meaning of her name. *Turn to page 140 and start reading at the Christmas tree.*

 We meet a precocious child who has all the right things to say. *Turn to page 142 and start reading at the gingerbread man.*

 Chrissy and Nick have the sobering realization that they may have rushed into this? *Turn to page 145 and start reading at the snowflake.*

 Kris, the mysterious old man from Candy Cane Falls who no one seems to realize is Santa Claus even though he dresses like him and says a lot of mysterious, holiday-magic-sounding things, makes a meaningful reappearance. *Turn to page 150 and start reading at the bow.*

BUILD YOUR OWN CHRISTMAS MOVIE ROMANCE

"Hey," said Nick, sidling up alongside her as if he had read her thoughts.

"Hey," Chrissy said, blushing. It had been a week since the rescue. It was no longer appropriate to be blushing. She was beginning to be concerned that this was a medical issue.

"You know," Nick said, "I was thinking. We're perfect for each other. How did it take us this long to finally get together?"

Chrissy paused and thought. Sometimes these questions don't have clear, easy answers. That being said, she did remember something about how even in high school, she had had this nagging, deep-seated sense that if they ever got together, they would prove to be incompatible on a cellular level and that, no matter how strong or undeniable their attraction to each other was, nothing either of them ever did or could ever do would possibly change that. Or … maybe it was just a timing issue? It was definitely one or the other.

"I don't remember," Chrissy said, smiling. She would deal more with those thoughts later.

"Hey," said Nick. "There's something I've been meaning to tell you. Actually, there's something I've been meaning to tell all of you."

He clinked his knife against his glass.

"Attention, everyone!" he shouted. "Attention, please!"

The room slowly grew quiet.

"Speech!" someone called from the back. There were scattered chuckles.

Nick climbed up on one of the dining room chairs and took a breath.

"As some of you may know," he began, "This beautiful woman to my left has been my girlfriend since I pulled her out of a freezing lake with a rope made of uncut candy canes."

Everyone nodded. A tale as old as time.

"But what some of you may *not* know," he continued, "is that in a far-off land, there is an old prophecy that goes like this: 'The one who is saved by a string of mint / To her will come an engagement.' That land is known as the Mentha Balsamea Isles. It is a real country, so do not look it up."

"Are you sure?" someone called from the crowd.

"It sounds vaguely European, doesn't it?" Nick countered.

There was a general murmur of agreement. That *was* the basic rule for what was considered a country.

"Well, I've never heard of it," Chrissy's mom said.

"Well, have you heard of *all* the countries?" Nick asked. "How do you do on *Jeopardy!* when it's a World Geography category?"

Chrissy's mom nodded. He had a point. That was one of her weaker categories, right up there with Lakes and Rivers, and Potent Potables.

"As I was saying," Nick continued, "the Mentha Balsamea Isles are real, and I should know, because …"

He ripped off the latex face mask he had been wearing this whole time—the one that made him look like he was clean-shaven—and revealed his true face, which basically looked exactly like his fake face, but it had a beard. The crowd gasped, and then applauded. Later, it would occur to most of them that a more cost-effective disguise would have been for Nick to just … shave.

> **"So I think that it is now obvious that I am secretly a prince."**

"So I think that it is now obvious that I am secretly a prince," Nick said, pointing to his beard.

He turned to Chrissy.

"I'm sorry for deceiving you," he said. "This whole time, you've known me as Nick, but the truth is, " he took a deep breath, "…my full name is actually Prince Nickington the Blizzardborn of House Music, Somehow 19th of His Name, Keeper

of the Goal, Leader of the Pack, the Unturnt, Breaker of Wind, and Father of Harrison. And you," he said, smiling at Chrissy, "are the fulfillment of the prophecy."

Chrissy slowly nodded. It was all starting to make sense. The strong, regal way Nick carried himself. The way he was always accidentally asking, "Where's my crown?" And how sometimes, when he was sitting in a reclining chair, he would open his mouth, point toward it, and say, "Grapes, please!"

"So," Nick said, reaching out his hand to Chrissy. "Will you come live in the Mentha Balsamea Isles with me? Will you be my queen and help rule our people forever? And will you also remind me to pick up Harrison from the babysitters' before we go? Because honestly I keep forgetting about him."

Chrissy took a deep breath. Was it really such a shock that she was the fulfillment of the prophecy from the minty islands place or wherever? She had all the qualities a great queen must possess: fine with wearing nude heels, safer driving in between armored cars, not a lot going on stateside. She could do this, Chrissy realized. She could actually do this.

She smiled and grabbed Nick's hand.

"I will," she said.

The room burst into cheers, and a chant broke out. "Chrissy! And Nick! Are prince! And princess! And maybe! King and queen! Later on! Depending!"

I didn't say it was a good chant.

Tears welled in Chrissy's eyes.

"This is the best Christmas ever," she whispered to Nick.

"Is that at least partially because you have historically hated Christmas because of your association between the holiday and your father and your imagined culpability in his death?" Nick whispered back.

"No!" Chrissy whispered. "Actually yes, that's a good point."

It didn't matter. This Christmas was a good Christmas. You might say that this Christmas was … royally good.

"Please don't say things like that," Nick whispered.

Chrissy hadn't realized that she had said that last part out loud.

Nick shook his head. There was only one way to stop her from making more terrible puns. He scooped her up, and they kissed.

"King me," Nick thought to himself. He knew he had just shot down Chrissy's royal pun, he thought, but come on. The *king me* thing was a good one. He was going to save that until a conversation about checkers came up, and then act like he had just come up with it on the spot. He smiled.

It really was a good Christmas.

The End

Just then, there was a sharp rap on the door. Chrissy couldn't imagine who it might be; it seemed as though the whole town was already in her mom's living room. Still, she walked to the front door and pulled it open.

Outside stood a woman who looked almost exactly like her. Looking at her face, Chrissy realized, was like looking into a mirror. Staring at the woman, she wondered: Is this really what I look like? Like a knock-off celebrity? Like the generic brand of, say, Blake Lively, who producers love because she costs significantly less to book? Chrissy shook her head; this was something to think about later. It was clear her doppelgänger had something to say.

"My name is Noel," said the doppelgänger breathlessly. "And I don't have much time to explain. But I need everyone at this party to come with me to the town square. Right away."

Something in the tone of her voice made Chrissy realize she was serious. Probably the serious tone.

"Okay," Chrissy said. "But what should I tell everyone I need them for?"

"Justice," Noel said solemnly.

This sounded important.

"Hey, everyone," Chrissy yelled back toward the kitchen where most of the guests had been gathering. "Get your coats and shoes on! We need to go to the town square … for justice!"

A big cheer went up.

Chrissy turned back to Noel and shrugged. "I guess it's that point in the evening where everyone is ready for justice," she said.

As the group of partygoers marched through the snow in a long line behind Noel and Chrissy, Noel tried to quickly summarize the situation.

"You aren't aware of what's been going," she explained to Chrissy, "because we don't know each other. But while you've been having your whole Christmas crisis, I've been having one of my own. It's a very long story, but here are the basics: I own a beloved ornament shop in the middle of town. It belonged to my grandfather, who raised me, so on top of being the sole source of income for my son and me, it's also a sentimental piece of property."

Chrissy nodded. She knew the place Noel was referring to: Ho-Ho-Hornaments. It was a terrible name, but a wonderful store, beloved by all the townspeople. So beloved, Chrissy thought, that it would be unequivocally tragic if a soulless real-estate conglomerate bought the land out from under the shop so that it could knock the building down and build luxury condos in its place.

"But a few weeks ago," Noel continued, "a soulless real-estate conglomerate told us it had bought the land from under the shop so that it could knock the building down and build luxury condos in its place."

Chrissy gaped. It was unequivocally tragic.

"Anyway," Noel said, speeding up her pace, "when Declan Halls, the representative for the soulless real-estate conglomerate, came to town, I knew right away what kind

"I have made my choice, Mr. Munneybaghs," he said, staring his boss in the eyes.

of person I was dealing with: He was heartless, cruel, seemingly driven entirely by money. But after weeks of bickering and tension between us—we fought like brother and sister, almost, especially like a brother who was both attracted to and trying to financially ruin his sister—there was a series of complicated and highly unlikely circumstances that slowly softened his heart, which eventually led to his somehow directing the school Christmas play, and as codirectors—yes, I also was inexplicably involved with the play, as I'm sure you've already guessed—he and I had a very romantically charged moment on stage while line-reading for Mary and Joseph, and ever since then, it's just kind of felt like our differences might actually be … our strength? Anyway, at the very least, I thought he had softened up enough that he might actually call the whole demolition off. But then his out-of-town boss showed up out of nowhere, and it seemed like Declan was suddenly torn between his old life and his new life, so he and I got into a huge fight, and he stormed out, and I haven't heard from him since."

Chrissy nodded. New life versus old life was very classic.

"And tonight," Noel explained, "is the scheduled demolition. The wrecking ball is waiting outside Ho-Ho-Hornaments. And I'm afraid that in order to prove his loyalty to his evil boss, Declan is going to man the demolition himself."

"So where do we come in?" Chrissy asked, gesturing vaguely at the huge group of partygoers marching in the snow behind them.

"If Declan is going to do this," Noel concluded somberly, "I'm at least going to make him look into the eyes of the townspeople whose lives he is destroying."

Her timing was perfect: Just as she finished her thought, Noel, Chrissy, and the entire group found themselves standing in the town square. There, to their left, stood the cheery exterior of Ho-Ho-Hornaments. And parked right in front of it stood a terrifying, massive crane. And even though the crane was covered in a large tarp for protection from the snow, it was immediately clear that this was the kind of crane that held a wrecking ball.

A handsome man stood next to the crane, looking nervous. They had arrived when he was mid-speech.

"And so," the handsome man continued, gesturing toward the crane, "I think it is clear I have made my choice."

"That's Declan," Noel whispered to Chrissy, pointing at the handsome man. "He's the one I was telling you about."

Next to Declan stood a man with a pencil-sharp moustache wearing an insulated, fur-lined tuxedo and chuckling evilly. "This is exactly why I hired you, Declan," he said, rubbing his hands together greedily. "I knew you'd come to your senses. Now let's tear off that tarp."

Looking nervous, Declan nodded and grabbed hold of the tarp. He took a deep breath.

"I *have* made my choice, Mr. Munneybaghs," he said, staring his boss in the eyes. "And this is my choice."

He ripped the tarp from the crane. The crowd gasped.

Because what they could see now is that there *was* a ball suspended at the top of the tall, yellow crane. But it wasn't a wrecking ball. It was a massive, wrecking-ball sized Christmas ornament. The crowd burst into cheers.

Declan turned to the crowd and searched out Noel's eyes.

"I choose Christmas," he said, and then the two rushed into each other's arms.

On the walk back to the house, Chrissy linked arms with her mom.

"That would have been a fun narrative to experience," Chrissy admitted.

"It would have," her mom agreed. Just then, it started to snow.

"A perfect evening," Chrissy said, smiling.

"And here I was, thinking we wouldn't have a white Christmas," her mom replied. "I guess it's just like my favorite Henry Ford quote says: 'Weather! You think you can, or you think you can't.'"

"You're right," Chrissy said.

"And hey, at least another person learned that business is bad tonight. That's a win in my book," her mother added.

Chrissy smiled and nodded, squeezing her mom's arm tight. These days, they really were in the business of hating business. And business … was good.

The End

"Oh my goodness!" Chrissy suddenly cried. "Cole, like *coal!*"

The End

"Have you tried the dip?" Chrissy's mom asked.

Chrissy surveyed the spread on the table. There were, by her estimation, 342 dips.

"Yes," she said truthfully. There had been 342 dips, and yes, she had tried them.

"I meant the spinach dip," her mom clarified. "It's a throwback to when I mentioned spinach dip on that phone conversation you and I had a while ago when you said you were going skiing on a mountain of gold or something instead of coming to this party. Do you remember?"

Chrissy thought. There were, by her estimation, 342 conversations her mom could be talking about.

"Yes," she said, mostly truthfully.

"Anyway," her mom said, "speaking of spinach dip. I've been meaning to tell you about the true meaning of your name."

"What do you mean?" asked Chrissy. "I already know the meaning of my name. I think it's even on the front of one of my baby books. What does it say again? Oh yeah: 'Chrissy: It's like Chris, but for a girl.' I always thought that was really meaningful."

Her mother smiled sadly.

"Your father wanted to wait until you were older to tell you your real name," she explained. "In fact, we were planning to tell you together, that night at the cabin, all those years back."

"What happened?" Chrissy asked. "Besides Dad dying, I mean."

"That morning," her mom said, "your dad pulled me aside and said, 'Chrissy cannot know the true meaning of her name until she has accepted that my impending death by snakebite was not her fault.' You know, as I say that out loud, I'm now realizing I should have maybe asked some follow-up questions, but your father was always having spooky premonitions, like, 'I think it's going to rain,' and 'Looks like the rain is going to die down.'"

"But what does 'Chrissy' mean?" Chrissy asked. "I think I'm ready to know."

"Chrissy means what you thought it did: Chris, but for a girl. But your name isn't Chrissy," her mom said, her eyes filling with tears. "Your real name … your whole name is … "

She started crying so hard she couldn't get the next word out.

"Christmas," Chrissy said softly, the realization slowly dawning on her. "My real name is Christmas."

Her mom nodded, wiping tears from her eyes.

"But wait," Chrissy gasped, looking up at her mom. "Your name. If my name is Christmas, and *your* name is …"

"Mary," her mom said quietly.

"Then together," Chrissy said gasping, "we're …"

"Christmas Mary," said Nick. He had come up behind Chrissy while she was talking. "By the way, speaking of Christmas, Mary," he said, looking at Chrissy's mom, "I rotated the dips for you so that the ones getting the least attention got moved to the front of the table so that they could be more accessible, and—"

"—would get the chance they deserved to be the star," Chrissy's mom whispered. "Thank you. You're a saint, Nick."

They all froze. That felt … meaningful?

"Christmas Mary," Nick said more loudly this time, putting his arms around Mary and Chrissy.

"Christmas Mary, indeed," Chrissy's mother said, smiling. Outside, church bells began to ring. It was midnight, and officially Christmas.

Christmas Merry indeed.

The End

Suddenly, Chrissy felt a tap on her leg. She looked down. Staring up at her was a scrawny little boy with cartoonishly large eyes. He wore a backpack, shorts held up by a smart pair of suspenders, and one of those rainbow hats with the spinners on top.

"Pardon me, ma'am," he said to Chrissy. "But I was hoping you could direct me to the water closet. If it isn't too much trouble."

Chrissy gaped. Oh my goodness, she thought. What luck. She had stumbled upon a precocious child.

> *"What is Heart of Darkness by Joseph Conrad? It's the right answer one out of ten times."*

"Water closet?" she asked. "Do you mean bathroom? Where did you learn the term 'water closet'?"

"Well," the little boy said, shoving a pair of horn-rimmed glasses up his nose, "It's simply a matter of preference. The term 'bathroom' is fine until you're talking about a half-bath, in which case, it's grossly inaccurate. I guess it's just that compared to American English, I simply find European terminology to be a bit less … crass."

"Crass," Chrissy repeated. "Who taught you that word? Aren't you like … six?"

The boy sighed. "I see I've done it again," he said. "I know I have a big vocabulary for my age. People are always saying that. I can tell they're teasing. But I guess that since I grew up without a mom, in a way …" He paused, taking off his backpack, unzipping it, and pulling out a large dictionary. "In a way," he continued, pointing at the cover, "this dictionary has been my mom. Does that make sense?"

"Yes," Chrissy said slowly, though it absolutely did not make sense. She was just distracted by how precocious he was.

"Say," said the little boy, "I've been thinking. And … Miss?" He gazed up at her again with those big, watery eyes. At that moment, he was so impossibly cute that Chrissy almost forgot that he definitely knew more words than her, and also, probably somehow, numbers. I want to adopt you, she found herself thinking. It would be good for her to have someone besides herself to take care of. And he would probably even teach her things like the difference between 'lay' and 'lie' and how to say the word 'oeuvre' without choking on her tongue and how to use the word *nonplussed* in a sentence that wasn't about subtraction problems.

"Would you … adopt me?" the little boy finished, as though he had read her thoughts.

She squatted down to look him in the eyes.

"Well, Harrison…" she said, then paused. "Your name *is* Harrison, right? I was just taking what felt like a very educated guess, considering just … everything you have going on, personality-wise."

Harrison nodded.

"Well, Harrison," she said, "I'd love to. I really would. You're everything I've ever wanted in a hypothetical child: You know big words, you already come with a cute hat. I would love the way your oversized vocabulary would reflect nicely on me, even though I would bear no responsibility for it. And I can't help but feel that I'd get better at *Jeopardy!* just by living in the same house as you."

Harrison nodded solemnly. "When in doubt," he said, "just guess, 'What is *Heart of Darkness* by Joseph Conrad?' It's the right answer one out of ten times."

"Exactly!" Chrissy exclaimed. "Stuff like that. But I'm afraid that I've recently entered into a very serious long-term relationship with a man who saved me from a frozen lake with a string of candy canes. And I hate to say this, but I just don't know if he's ready for us to adopt a child from a Christmas party." She gave the spinner at the top of his head a sad flick. "I'm sorry, buddy. I wish it could be different."

Just then, Nick walked up to the two of them. He put his arm around Chrissy.

"I see we're making friends!" he said cheerfully.

"Nick, this is Harrison," Chrissy said, at the same time as Harrison said, "Dad, this is Chrissy."

The three of them stared at each other. There was a lot of jaw dropping and pointing, and "Wait, what are you trying to tell me?" until they basically got it all sorted out.

"Well," Nick said, putting his arms around both of them. "I'd say your Christmas wish came true this year, didn't it, Harrison?"

Harrison looked confused.

"You don't have to hide it from me," Nick reassured him. "I found your folded-up Christmas list. All you had written on it was 'Mom.' You didn't have to be embarrassed, buddy. All you wanted for Christmas ... was a mom."

Harrison nodded slowly. "Oh ... yes," he said. "I remember." He didn't have the heart to tell his dad that if he had unrolled Harrison's Christmas list further, he would have seen that Harrison had not, in fact, written *Mom*, but had instead written *Momostenango Uncovered*, the title of a recently published book of facts about Momostenango, his favorite municipality in the Totonicapán department of Guatemala. More information about Momostenango: *that* was really all Harrison had wanted for Christmas.

But in the meantime, he thought, this stranger his dad had pulled out of a frozen lake with a rope of candy canes who now wanted to be his mom? He grinned. She would do just fine.

Plus, she could also probably buy him *Momostenango Uncovered.*

His smile grew. It was going to be—he shoved his glasses up his nose in triumph—an absolutely prodigious Christmas.

The End

There was just this one little issue, something that had been nagging her ever since Nick had rescued her from drowning in the lake. Like any reasonable person, she had always believed that if a handsome townie rescued her from a frozen lake using a jerry-rigged candy cane rope she would marry that person, right? It was the classic fantasy.

But was that actually what she wanted?

On top of that, there was the whole issue of her having been hearing mysterious, tinkling bells ever since she arrived in Candy Cane Falls. No one else could hear them, that much was clear, so she was either dealing with the beginnings of a descent into madness, or she was the chosen one in a mysterious, magical Christmas adventure yet to come. Either way, those felt like things she should do on her own, no boyfriends or husbands allowed. There was, she admitted to herself, the off chance that she was just dealing with tinnitus, in which case her marital status was probably inconsequential. But probably it was madness or magic stuff.

As if he read her mind, Nick sidled up beside her.

"Sure is magical, huh?" he asked.

She glanced at him.

"You and me, I mean," he explained. "It's hard to believe that before you got here, I was just a guy who had recently been fired from Violin Femmes, the local band I founded that did string-quartet covers of Limp Bizkit songs."

Chrissy looked confused.

"I know the name is a little confusing," Nick admitted. "Violin Femmes was just the only orchestral pun we could come up with. But to be very clear, we exclusively covered Limp Bizkit songs."

Chrissy was starting to feel a bit faint.

"Why were you kicked out of the band?" she asked. Suddenly, she was afraid to know.

"For loving Limp Bizkit too much," he admitted. "Everyone else in the band was doing it ironically, I guess, but I was 100 percent genuinely into them, and once that became clear, it was a deal breaker. But what can I say? I don't have any regrets. In the end, I did it all for the—"

"Cookie?" Chrissy's mom asked. She was holding a tray of Christmas cookies.

"No, Mom, thank you," Chrissy said, waving her off. She was too busy having a series of epiphanies.

"Nick," she said, "if I left my city life behind and moved to Candy Cane Falls to be with you, what would we do?"

"What do you mean?" Nick laughed. "We'd sit in twin rocking chairs on the front porch, holding mittened hands and watching the sunset on the glistening, candy cane–dotted horizon."

"And then?" Chrissy asked.

"And then," Nick said, "I assume I would give your hand a squeeze, and you'd give my hand a squeeze, and we'd both give the other a meaningful smile, and then we'd get back to looking at the snow while the credits rolled."

"The credits?"

"The figurative credits," Nick said.

"What are figurative credits?" Chrissy asked.

"I don't know," Nick said. "I guess like when you kind of methodically think through all the important people in your life and the roles that they've played in order of significance?"

"But after that," Chrissy said. "What would we do for like, jobs?"

"I saved you from a lake," Nick said.

"And what about friends? My whole life is in New York."

BUILD YOUR OWN CHRISTMAS MOVIE ROMANCE

"You accidentally fell on top of me in a candy cane field and there was tension," Nick continued.

"And don't you think that it's maybe possible for me to experience personal growth without also throwing away the career and life that I've spent years building?"

"Abs?" Nick said, confused, pulling his shirt up slightly.

"All I'm saying," Chrissy said, "is that maybe we don't actually know each other that well and should, at the very least, slow things down and do the distance thing. Like, at absolute most."

"But," Nick stammered, "we pulled candy canes out of the ground together."

"I know," said Chrissy, "and for most people, that would be enough to build a life on. But while I'm happy to have experienced some personal growth over the past few weeks in Candy Cane Falls, I also don't know that I necessarily accept what I feel that our storyline is implying, which is that living in a big city is categorically a moral failing."

Nick sighed and nodded.

"I get it," he said. "It's like the guys in Violin Femmes once said to me: 'Go away, Nick, you like Limp Bizkit too much.' Maybe you're my Limp Bizkit."

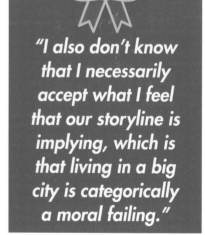

"I also don't know that I necessarily accept what I feel that our storyline is implying, which is that living in a big city is categorically a moral failing."

Chrissy shuddered.

"Nick," she said, "that's sincerely such a huge bummer to hear you say. But I think it also tells me everything I need to know."

She stuck out her hand.

"Friends?" she asked. "And absolutely nothing more?"

Nick clasped her hand.

"Friends," he agreed. "But can I say one more thing before you go?"

Chrissy nodded.

He sighed.

"I just want to say," he started, "that after everything, I ... I need some time off from that emotion. Time to pick my heart up off the floor when that love comes down."

"Wow, Nick," Chrissy said, impressed. "That's actually beautiful. Did you just come up with that?"

"Oh, I wish," laughed Nick. "That's from a little song called 'Faith.'"

"Oh, no," said Chrissy.

"By the band Limp Bizkit," said Nick.

"Yes, I got that," said Chrissy. "This has been clarifying. Goodbye, Nick."

"Goodbye, Chrissy," Nick said.

Chrissy turned to leave, but Nick stopped her.

"Just one more thing," he said, reaching into his back pocket and producing a candy cane. He held it out toward her.

"If you ever want to hook up," he said, pointing at the hooked end of the candy cane, "call me."

Chrissy looked at him blankly.

"Get it?" Nick said, pointing at the candy cane again. "Like because it's a hook."

"No, again, I got it," said Chrissy. "Goodbye." This time, she really did walk away.

When she was at the front door, she looked back and saw Nick, already joking cheerfully with a group of guests from the party. The two of them were going to be just fine, Chrissy realized with a smile. Then she saw Nick grab a brand-new carton of eggnog and open it just using the divots between his abs. She winced. Leaving was the right thing to do, but still: Nick with the eggnog was a lot to process, both emotionally and logistically.

She was still sorting through the emotional wreckage of that image as she walked outside and onto the porch. A light snow had just begun to fall. It was the perfect Christmas evening.

Chrissy collapsed into the porch swing and sat there for a long while. She didn't always like to admit it, but Candy Cane Falls truly was beautiful at night. With a smile, she realized that for the first time in a long while, she wasn't in a hurry to be anywhere. For the first time in a long while, she was perfectly fine right where she was.

Which was good because she didn't have a car.

The End

And she really was enjoying it, she thought to herself. That's when she realized what she really wanted, more than anything, right in that moment: to be able to be everywhere at the party all at once. Because in that moment, she was feeling so fondly toward every single person in Candy Cane Falls that she wanted to be with all of them at once—to be a part of every conversation, of every hug, of every shared smile and clinked glass. She almost wished, she realized, that she was in a movie, so that the camera could zoom out a little, letting her magically see into every room at the same time, each one full of people enjoying the simple pleasure of a Christmas party in her childhood home.

And if the camera could have zoomed out even farther, she would have been able to see her parents' beautiful home from above, its windows glowing brightly, the snowy yard dotted with trees, the newly harvested candy cane fields out back clean and bare.

If the camera could have zoomed out farther than that, then she would have seen her house as just one of dozens of tiny, glowing houses on her street; and if it zoomed out even farther than that, she would have seen the entire town of Candy Cane Falls, every tiny shop and sign accounted for; and if the camera had zoomed out just a bit farther, she would have seen that the whole tiny town was contained inside of a delicate snow globe, her house now just one bright speck among dozens of other warm, bright specks underneath a glass dome.

And if she could have zoomed out just a bit farther than that, she would have seen Kris, reclining in a comfortable, overstuffed chair, looking down at the miniature town of Candy Cane Falls inside of his snow globe warmly. She would have seen him wind the key on the snow globe, set it down, and close his eyes as the sound of tinkling bells began to play. And if she had waited a few more moments after that, she would have seen him open his eyes, grin directly into the camera, and wink.

The End